KU-645-232

CONTENTS

INTRODUCTION 7

TOOLS OF THE TRADE: 9

ROMANCE 31

SCIENCE FICTION 50

WESTERN 70

CRIME 96

HORROR 134

FANTASY 154

THRILLER/ADVENTURE 176

CHICK LIT 200

MEMOIR 220

CHILDREN'S 221

GETTING IT OUT THERE: 222

Just Write

Gabrielle Mander

This edition first published in Great Britain by

Virgin Books Ltd
Thames Wharf Studios
Rainville Road
London W6 9HA

With special thanks to Carola Campbell

Designed and typeset by Design 23
Printed in the UK by CPI Bookmarque, Croydon, CR0 4TD

INTRODUCTION

You have a book inside you, everyone has a book inside them, or so they say, but how do you get that story out of your head and down on paper?

Just write it! That's all very well, I hear you say, but I can't write, I can talk alright, but all those rules of grammar, and spelling, plot and characterization, every time I think about it, I remember school and close my notebook or laptop and give up. Many famous writers have said that the hardest part is getting started, getting those first words down. They may be rejected later, but, like the famous journey of 1000 miles that starts with but a single step, a number one, million-copy bestseller starts with but a single word.

Just Write is a unique collection of beginnings and endings of stories to inspire you. They are free for you to use as a basis for your own stories, or just to read for fun to get your brain working. Each kind of popular fiction is here: romance, chick-lit, crime, thriller/adventure, western, horror, science fiction and fantasy plus guidance for children's stories and personal memoirs. Hints and tips on how to go about writing different kinds of fiction are included. Each kind has its own set of buzzwords – a bank of phrases, vocabulary and, where appropriate, even characteristic names, commonly used in each genre, to get you in the mood. *Just Write* also includes hints on research and using the internet, blogging and ebooks, and ideas about plots and characters and gives some professional advice on finding an agent, reading contracts and catching and keeping your very own publisher.

All of us may not get published, we may not write the great novel of the 21st century, but your words and language and your unique and boundless imagination belong to you, and you are free and entitled to use them to tell your stories, for your own pleasure or therapy, as well as to share with others. Just write!

TOOLS OF THE TRADE

One of the many wonderful things about writing is that you can do it anywhere, although some writers like to have a base from which to write, to which they can return knowing that everything is exactly as they left it (sharpened pencils standing in pots), and in which they feel comfortable. It can also be useful, though by no means essential, to have a space that your family and friends understand to be off limits, and in which you are not to be disturbed.

You do not need complicated equipment, or even any experience to get started. If your grammar and spelling are a bit rusty, or your education failed to equip you with the basics, don't despair; that is easily solved. What you do need is the desire to write your stories down, if only for yourself. Each of us remembers what it was like to be a child, when we were not embarrassed to invent games, imaginary friends, and in fact whole worlds for ourselves. All of us sleep and dream at night, when our subconscious reorganises our thoughts and experiences into free movies, each with their own logic, untrammelled by convention. Every one of us has the potential to be creative. Some already express that creativity through their homes, in designing their own environment and some through food and cooking, others through their personal appearance and how they dress. Still others create beautiful flower gardens or grow mouth-watering vegetables. There are many ways to channel our creative urges, but writing, like painting and music can be especially satisfying and a means to share your thoughts, ideas and experiences with other people. It is also extremely therapeutic. Just try featuring a faithless partner or bullying boss in a little scenario of your own creation, or writing a harmless fictional outcome for your difficult day (possibly involving carnage and mayhem), and you will see what I mean.

Sadly, a lot of us have locked our creativity away with the toys and games of our childhood. The aim of this book is to provide new writers with a bunch of skeleton keys to unlock the doors to their own imaginations. *Just Write* definitely does not presume to be a creative writing course. There are many excellent courses and resources to develop your skills, which you can access through your library, local authority or online. For some of us, these can seem daunting and reminiscent of school and of being judged. Actually, most are not like that and can be great places to meet other writers and share ideas and swap problems too. In any event, you don't have to start with a formal course. Even the creative process of preparing to write can be very entertaining in its own right, whether anything actually finds its way on to paper or not, so why not give it a try in those in-between times in your busy life. The writer's toolbox will hardly weigh you down. The following list could be enough to see you through any project, from a love letter to *War and Peace*. (Although, Tolstoy has already written that, so you might want to try *Warp and Peas*, an original work of science fiction, about the difficulties of eating small green pulses at speeds faster than the speed of light).

You will need:
- Your own imagination.
- Time to write.
- Time to read other people's work, especially that which inspires or entertains you.
- Your personal experiences, or those of others as told to you.

- Background reading and detailed research.
- A selection of pens and paper or notebooks, or a typewriter or computer.
- A good dictionary (don't rely on online dictionaries).
- A good thesaurus (don't rely on online sources). If you have never used one of these books of lists of synonyms for the many words in English that mean roughly the same thing, depending on how you use them, you have a treat in store. A thesaurus is such a great refuge when you are stuck for a word, and will help you to avoid repetition in your text. It is also handy for cheating at crossword puzzles.
- A good dictionary of simile and metaphor.
- A grammar crib sheet or small book, just for reassurance and to remind you of those pesky rules of grammar and punctuation. (See page 24 for the absolute basics.)
- A library card. (Libraries are magnificent free resource centres and will order books for you).
- Ideas, a pocket notebook and pen to jot them down or to sketch descriptive passages when they occur to you. Sometimes a tiny incident observed from the top of a bus, or a description of a person glimpsed in the street can inspire you and find its way into your work years later. Dreams, or newspaper stories are also good sources of inspiration, as are overheard snatches of conversation. Write them down.
- Powers of observation. Practise describing events or people in minute detail. A series of headings can sometimes help

  Appearance:
  Size:

Weight:
Ethnic origin:
Colour of hair:
Colour of eyes:
Approximate age:
Clothes:
Manner of walking or moving:
(or posture, it is a great indicator of state of mind)
Accessories:
Distinguishing features:

Imagine that you are asked, as a witness, to give a detailed description to the police, following some kind of incident. You don't have to write it all down, although that is most useful, just catalogue these things in your head, but let it become a habit as you go about your daily life. When you do spot something you would like to record, or when you need to access your own memory files for a person, or event that is perfect in the context of your current piece of work, close your eyes, and register the sounds, smells and sensations surrounding the event. Can you feel the sun on your face? Are you warm or cold? Can you hear rain, or traffic, footsteps or birdsong? Can you smell exhaust fumes, or scents like perfume, wet wool, soap or shampoo? Open your eyes and write down the detail. Consider the light; is it natural or artificial? What is the season? Is the weather cloudy or clear? Is it so cold you can see your breath in front of your face, or so hot that you can taste salty sweat when you lick your lips? Write it all down. One day you might want to place your characters in a similar scene.

Most of us have to spend time waiting in a public place, an airport or doctor's waiting room, or a station or hotel foyer.

Amuse yourself by making up back stories for the people around you; just from the clues you get from their physical appearance. That chap over there for instance, he must be sixty, but his hair is still a luxuriant black. Why? Does he colour it, if so why? Perhaps he is trying to attract a young lover, or is worried that his boss might notice that he is getting older and start to ease him out of his job? He could be an ardent Elvis fan who has read that 'the king' dyed his hair black to the end of his days and is copying his idol. What about that woman in the next seat who is holding her newspaper some distance away and screwing up her eyes? Why isn't she wearing spectacles or contact lenses? Did she forget them? Was her luggage stolen and with it, the spectacles? Is she just too vain to admit she needs spectacles? Perhaps she can't afford the cost? Perhaps she is feigning interest in the newspaper and it doesn't matter to her that she can't read it properly? Maybe she is a private detective on surveillance? Could she be an alien in human form, whose eyes are not correctly adjusted for reading? The possibilities, which stem from one tiny observation, are endless. Exercising your imagination, and indeed writing, is like any other skill, the more you practise the better at it you will become, and you don't have to start with a 100, 000 word novel.

Research has suggested that many would-be writers don't write because they assume that they will not be good enough. Why do they think this? Usually, insensitive teachers have criticised their language or grammatical skills at an early age, or they have been teased by friends and family for even attempting to express themselves on paper. It is also true that many creative people leap from the seed of an idea, to imagining fame and riches and interviews on talk shows. They sit down at their computers or pick up a pen and start to write. Then they experience a huge confidence crisis. Can they write enough? Will anyone like what they write? Where should the punctuation marks come? Will they be rejected etc. etc? Do not be put off by fear of failure and do not expect to win literary prizes and wind up in the gossip columns. Both or neither may happen, so the following tip is vital. In the first instance, forget about publication; forget about possible errors, they can be corrected. Write your story for yourself, and the pleasure it will give you, and you will undoubtedly discover that you are your own fiercest critic.

Structure

The building blocks for any story are narrative, character, and plot.

Narrative

This is simply the story you have to tell and the style in which you tell it. This will include the pace at which your story moves, the way you introduce tension and the actual narrative style you choose. It can be useful, especially if you are more used to television or movie drama than the written word, to imagine your story as a film, in which you can cut between camera shots: close ups on the main characters, point of view shots from the narrator or subsidiary characters, panoramic shots which give an overview of the current state of play, action shots which move the plot along and tracking shots that follow first one character and then another. Now translate that into writing. Consider using different 'voices' to vary the pace. Try to end each chapter without resolving the action – a cliffhanger, so to speak, to create tension. Then start the next chapter in a calmer mood, from a different part of the narrative, or with a different character. The reader must read through to discover what transpired in the previous chapter. You must also decide whether your story is to be written in the first person, like, for example, The *Lovely Bones* or in the third person, like *Pride and Prejudice.*

Other decisions will involve choosing a style in which to tell the story. For example you could choose a straightforward narrative, or write it in the form of a diary, or a correspondence between two protagonists. Perhaps it is a collection of newspaper reports, or a deathbed confession. You may need to try out several different styles before you find the right way in which to tell your own story.

Character

The observational exercises above will be very useful when it comes to developing characters. When you begin it is a good idea to limit the number to perhaps five leading characters, of which one of two will be principal. You are going to need to keep track of each of your creations, their life stories, personality traits and foibles, as well as their actions, and you can't just forget about a few and leave them on a bus somewhere. Each character's part in the story needs to be resolved. Your protagonists and antagonists need to be credible, although not necessarily likeable. Your reader needs to be interested in what they do, and why they do it and to identify with them to some degree, especially with heroes and heroines. Your main characters will also need other people, secondary characters with whom to interact, and who can help move the plot along. Detective fiction provides a perfect example. Where would Poirot be without poor Captain Hastings, or Holmes without Dr

Watson to patronise, or Miss Marple without the dim-witted or admiring policemen in every story? These characters not only have lives and roles of their own, they also ask the questions, or react to situations, on behalf of the reader. Sometimes they influence our feelings about the main character. Dr Watson, for example seems remarkably fond of Holmes. He admires his genius for detection of course, but there is also a hint that he is aware of events in Holmes' life which account for his less attractive idiosyncrasies, and that he tolerates these for this reason. Watson is such a thoroughly decent chap that if he likes Holmes, we feel that perhaps we should too. Sidekicks are very useful characters to invent.

Other characters may be devised to add texture and context to the plot, or exist just as red herrings. Allegedly, there is a tradition in theatre, especially opera, known as 'fifth business'. Fifth business is someone who is a seemingly unimportant, an odd character out, with perhaps only a word here, or an action there, but who is in fact essential to the plot and to the resolution of the story. Remember 'fifth business', it is very handy.

Character chart

Many writers find it useful to create a chart for each character, a kind of questionnaire, (have a look at an online dating questionnaire for inspiration) which the writer fills in on his or her behalf. These should be finely detailed, beginning with physical appearance, likes and dislikes, interests, motivation, family background, siblings, childhood experiences, friends, the kind of food, music, hobbies etc that he or she prefers. What is his voice like? What kind of car would he drive? Is she introvert or extrovert? Personality traits and foibles feature too, and psychological profiles of how these habits and characteristics have been formed. Ask yourself why your character hates water, or is passionate about poetry for example, and write down the answer.

You may never describe these traits in your story, but you will know about them, and that knowledge will influence the way you describe a related scene. What are his or her other strengths and weaknesses? The inclusion of human flaws, to which we are all subject, will make him or her believable, and help the reader to empathise. When you get to know and understand your character and what motivates him or her, you will direct his dialogue and actions in character. Your understanding of your character's fear of water for example, will enhance your description of his courage in rescuing a drowning child, moments before he tumbles over the weir. Writers often say that their characters develop a life of their own once they hit the page, and it is important to keep control of them and make them behave as the reader will come to expect. When you describe events from their points of view, you are like an actor who has to play all the parts in this story and get under the skin of each. This may sound like hard work, but in fact it is great fun, and an important part of the creative process. God is in the detail.

Plot

Novels are, on the whole, said to be either plot or character-driven. In the former, you have an idea of a sequence of events, which will lead to the climax of the novel and you need to create characters capable of performing the necessary actions convincingly, to drive your narrative. In the latter, you know that your main protagonist is to be, for example, an introverted thirty-five-year-old man with a dog, and you need to make him take actions and interact with other characters to reveal the plot. In truth, most novels are a mixture, and at their best, whatever the genre, they will tell us more about the human condition. They will also entertain or move us, frighten or enlighten us, but it is paramount that they engage us from the start.

The Beginning

To that end, so to speak, the beginning of a novel should never be too long. It should introduce the reader to the theme of the story, settle quickly into the context in which the narrative takes place, introduce the main characters and let the reader know what to expect of them. The opening line of any novel is crucial. If you are a genius, like the authors below, you might come up with a first line, which both grabs attention and saves pages of scene setting and explanation. What is certain is that each knew exactly what was going to happen in the climax of the book and could evoke the spirit and intention of the entire novel in their opening lines.

'It was the best of times, it was the worst of times'
CHARLES DICKENS, *A Tale of Two Cities*

'It is a truth universally acknowledged that a single man in possession of a good fortune must be in want of a wife"
JANE AUSTEN, *Pride and Prejudice*

'Call me Ishmael.'
HERMAN MELVILLE, *Moby Dick*

'The past is a foreign country. They do things differently there.'
L P HARTLEY, *The Go-Between*

'It was a bright, cold day in April, and the clocks were striking thirteen.'
GEORGE ORWELL, *1984*

'It was the day my grandmother exploded.'
IAIN BANKS, *The Crow Road*

'My name was Salmon, like the fish; first name Susie. I was fourteen when I was murdered on December 6, 1973.'
ALICE SEBOLD, *The Lovely Bones*

'If you really want to hear about it, the first thing you'll probably want to know is where I was born, and what my lousy childhood was like, and how my parents were occupied and all before they had me, and all that David Copperfield kind of crap, but I don't feel like going into it, if you want to know the truth.'?
J.D. SALINGER, *The Catcher in the Rye*

If you are not confident of your genius and your ability to hold a plot in your head, as well as the qualities, foibles and descriptions of every character, and then sum the whole up in the opening line, you might find the following device useful.

Plotline
A plotline is a chart or table, along the length of which you mark the key events of the narrative at intervals. If your story is plot-driven, your plotline may well start with the ending. You know

what is going to happen, in sequence, to reach your pre-determined conclusion and you will create the right characters to act out your story and present your theme engagingly. If Tolstoy had devised a plotline for *War and Peace,* for example (no easy task!) it might include actions such as 'The army is defeated and retreats from Moscow' 'the retreating troops pass through a remote village', 'the wounded man is discovered' etc. (with apologies to Tolstoy for this not very accurate representation of the plot of *War and Peace*)

Your plotline is event led, and you will need to develop a clear idea of the kind of characters who would initiate or represent the actions, to take you through the stages of the plot, from the setting, through the crisis, to the climax. You will also need to create a timeline in which these events can occur, and you will have to set a location in which these are actually geographically possible. You will assign suitable characters to your actions to bring events about, or push the narrative through.

Even if your narrative is character-driven, you could still find it useful to devise a plotline to anchor the characters in the plot and plan the action. Where will your story take place, who will interact with your main characters, what are their stories and so on? But in this event you might like to start at the beginning. 'Pierre, the handsome, tortured war correspondent feels that he must leave for Moscow – leaves Sept 10th', 'Meets Natasha, beautiful wife of Prince Andre, whom he has known since she was a child, in a remote village' 'the simple farm lad discovers the body in the hand-cart, and so on.' In a character-driven novel, you are inventing events that will give your characters a stage on which to perform, and the plot will be revealed through them and the narrative is taken forward.

When you have settled on your narrative, plotted your plotline and devised your characters, you will be ready to plan the three main stages of the book. The beginning, the crisis and the climax, and you will need to set a pace for the whole that will keep the reader engaged. In the beginning, the scene is set and we meet the main characters. In the next third of the book a series of events, each caused by the last, will lead the characters to a crisis-point. During the crisis, both the characters and the plot will deepen and move towards the last third, the climax, which will, by definition, resolve all the issues for both the characters and the reader in a satisfactory way.

Research

It is absolutely vital, if your story is to be successful, that you do detailed and painstaking research into the subject and the period in which it is set. Dissonance will jar and destroy both the reader's enjoyment and your credibility, and that of your characters. Do not allow them to say or do things that no one of their time or in their situation would ever do. This is especially true for historical settings and technical plots. We all know, for example, how irritating it is when a character in an historical film uses language or takes actions, which are impossible. 'Robin Hood, Prince of Thieves' was ruined for many at the outset, when the film opened as Robin and his companion arrived on the shore at Dover, on England's south coast and proceeded to walk to Nottingham, in the middle of the country and a distance of hundreds of miles, only to arrive on the same day!

Many readers, like filmgoers are huge fans of a particular genre and have encyclopaedic and expert knowledge of the subject. They will spot careless research instantly, and put your book aside contemptuously. For example, if you plonk your characters down in the middle of England in the nineteenth century, and only rail travel will move them into position in time for your plot to unfold, make sure you check the routes and timetables of railways in that period. If you say that a cop was born and brought up in Los Angeles, you can't have him talking like a New Yorker, from Brooklyn. If you are writing crime or science fiction, make sure you get the technical detail right. If in doubt, do not be too ambitious; follow the adage of writers throughout history and start by writing about what you know. Set your story in your own time and in the language that you speak and with which you are most comfortable, especially if you don't have the time or dedication to do the research. The buzzwords lists at the end of each genre in this book are not intended to replace research; they are merely to give you a flavour of the genre and its language, so that you can try it out. Don't rely on them; some are quite whimsical!

Please don't be put off by the work involved in creating credible and engaging fiction, it can be unbelievably rewarding, and whatever you write, enjoy the journey as well as looking forward to the destination.

Libel

Now there is a frightening word. Risk of litigation for libel can be avoided if you are scrupulous about two things. The first is making your work wholly original, and never using real people's names, or undisguised characters based on real people in your fiction. If you do, and your model can claim that their character has been defamed or that they have suffered in any way as a result, they could sue you. Secondly, do not use product placement in a derogatory way. If you use brand names at all, or even descriptions of products that could be identified with well-known brands, make sure that the way in which a product or location is used is sympathetic to that brand's image. For example, do not have slave labour in a third world country manufacturing well-known, named brands, unless you have first-hand incontrovertible evidence that this has taken place. The laws governing newspapers and books differ, since the latter is available for much longer than the former and unsubstantiated exposure cannot be said to be serving the public interest in a work of fiction, as a news item might. Libel laws also vary from country to country. If you are in any doubt, consult a libel lawyer and have your work read. This is a very cursory description. There are organisations, which supply resources to writers and run courses for publishers and editors. If you intend to be contentious, do get legal advice.

Copyright

Copyright is a very complex subject, and once again, if you are in any doubt, consult a copyright lawyer or take advice from a professional writers' organisation. But as a rule of thumb, an author needs to have been dead for 70 years for his or her work to be out of copyright and thus available to you for unlimited quotation. Even then, the copyright might have been assigned to an estate before the term was complete, so you need to check permissions before quoting substantive amounts of another author's work. Ownership of a physical object does not confer copyright. So, for example you might buy a magazine from the 1940s, containing a story, which you use as a basis for your own work. The magazine is long since out of print, and the publisher defunct, and you do not have a clear indication as to whom the copyright in the story belongs. If in doubt, and you are unable to confirm its ownership, do not use it. Where possible you should always obtain permission to quote other works and cite your sources, ascribing the copyright to the correct source. Most publishers will advise on copyright, but their contracts with authors will normally stipulate that it is the author's responsibility to clear all permissions. They may have work read for possible infringement of both libel and copyright laws, but remember that they are protecting themselves, not you, from lawsuits.

Be original, and keep scrupulous notes citing sources when you are copying pieces of text for research. It is very easy to come across a piece of text in a notebook, which expresses in perfect prose, all that you want to say, and to have forgotten that it was said first by Oscar Wilde or JK Rowling.

Basic grammar and punctuation in building a story

Take a **noun** or two (a noun is a name for something: e.g. cat, dog.)

A **proper noun** is a proper name: e.g. (Wiffles) the cat.
A **verb** is the action that that noun performs so Cat (noun) plays (verb) with dog (noun).

The **definite article** refers to one special noun so

The (definite article) cat plays with the (definite article) dog.

The **indefinite article** refers to any old noun so
A (indefinite article) cat plays with a (indefinite article) dog.
Do we care about any old cat and dog? We do not! So we are more likely to use the indefinite article when the sentence forms part of the background description, e.g. The park is almost deserted now. It is getting dark; a cat plays with a dog…

A **possessive pronoun** goes before the noun and owns it. Thus we have, my (his, her, your, their) (all possessive pronouns) cat etc.

An **adjective** describes a noun, and adds to its meaning.
My (possessive pronoun) beautiful (adjective) cat Wiffles,
plays (verb) with (possessive pronoun) your ugly (adjective) dog Jaws.

The addition of possessive pronouns, and adjectives to the nouns, not only describes what is actually happening, but adds value to the statement. We can deduce from that sentence, that I am a soppy cat owner, besotted with my animal and that I don't much care for your dog. I probably don't much care for you either, since I am insulting your dog quite freely.

If I add in a few more adjectives, My beautiful, pedigree cat, Wiffles, plays with your ugly, mongrel dog Jaws, I am now implying that I can afford a pedigree cat, whilst you only have a mongrel dog. I think that Jaws is beneath Wiffles and by extension, you are beneath me. I am a bit of an unpleasant snob. On the other hand, the reader might rather like you. You probably rescued your dog from a dog-pound and he is faithful unto death, whereas I purchased my inbred, unaffectionate, pampered pet as an accessory to my shallow and superficial life.

The power of a few words and a little imagination is extraordinary.

But I can alter this perception, with one or two strokes of the keyboard!

My beautiful, gentle, pedigree cat Wiffles, plays happily with your ugly, vicious, mongrel dog Jaws.

Now, my cat reflects well on me; she is brave and generous, not afraid of Jaws, but willing to give him the benefit of the doubt, despite appearances and a string of previous biting convictions. My cat and I are trusting and open. The addition of the two more adjectives and **an adverb** (happily), which describes how Wiffles plays,) will give that judgemental reader pause (or paws) for thought.

This seems pretty basic stuff, and do you really need to be reminded of the names of the parts of a sentence? Of course not, but it is useful to remind ourselves what those simplest of words can do for us, depending on how we choose and use them.

Obviously grammar is much complicated than that, what about dangling participles? I hear you cry. (What indeed?) But this is not a grammar primer. Incidentally proper names begin with capital letters. So does the personal pronoun I which stands instead of the proper name, e.g. Gabrielle wishes to state for the record, that she does not own, nor has she ever owned a pedigree cat called Wiffles; or I wish to state that I do not own, nor have I ever a owned a pedigree cat called Wiffles.

Q What is the difference between a cat and a sentence?
A. A cat has clawses at the end of its pawses, and a sentence has pauses at the end of its clauses.

Some Punctuation Basics

All sentences begin with a capital letter.

All sentences end with one of the following:
. ? ! A **full stop** (or period), a **question mark** or an **exclamation mark**.

. Full stop:	This grammar lesson is now over.
? Question mark:	(for when you require an answer)
	Are you glad this grammar lesson is now over?
! Exclamation mark:	I am delighted that this grammar lesson is now over!

, A **comma**, is used to indicate a short pause between two parts of a sentence; for example, to make reading more like natural speech, to separate items in a list of three or more items (except before 'and'), when addressing someone, or reporting what they said, to show that you have missed a word or words out, before but or for, to show contrast, where a phrase adds something new to the sentence, whether it is important to the meaning or not, where the main clause depends for its meaning on the preceding one, when you are addressing someone, and when the phase could be in brackets.

1. If your cat is chased, shout at the dog owner.
2. You will need: fish, meat, milk, litter and a bowl.
3. "George, please go and catch Wiffles."
   George replied, "Go and fetch Wiffles yourself."
4. Fool me once, shame on you, [fool me] twice, shame on me.

5.　The cat was not lost, but gone before
　　Though she was small, she was very brave.
　　She was small, with a thick coat, but she was brave.
8.　Mrs Smith, who loves cats, is taking driving lessons.
9.　Mary, please take Wiffles outside.
10.　The cat, which had a pedigree as long as your arm, teased the dog.

; A **semi-colon** marks a longer pause when the contents of the clause are tangential to the sentence, although important to it. It is also used in a list, which has commas already.

The cat seemed to like the dog; she purred when he approached.

A Tale of Two Cities, by Charles Dickens; *Pride and Prejudice*, by Jane Austen; *War and Peace*, by Leo Tolstoy and *The Catcher in the Rye* by JD Salinger are all great works of literature.

: A **colon** is used before a list and after a statement of fact.
You will need: fish, a bowl, meat and cat litter.

There was only one thing to do: run like the wind.

A **dash** can be used before a phrase that summarizes the idea of a sentence or before and after a phrase or list that adds extra information in the middle of a sentence. (In place of commas)

Small, cross and furry – these are the characteristics of Wiffles

The cats – Wiffles, Waffles, and George – were sisters and brother.

- A **hyphen** joins two words that form one idea together, joins prefixes to words and is used when writing compound numbers.
  sweet-smelling
  anti-establishment
  forty-three

' An **apostrophe** indicates one of two things; that the noun that follows belongs to someone or something, (the only exception is its) and when a letter or letters have been missed out, for example: 'was not' - wasn't, 'cannot' - can't, 'could not' - couldn't. In these cases it tells us that there should be another letter in these words, but we have removed it to contract the word. Other examples include, hadn't, haven't won't etc. This is the only time 'it's' should have an apostrophe: 'it is'. It's a fine day.

Apostrophes in the plural: If the possessive is in the singular describing something belonging to only one noun, e.g. The dog's dinner, it goes before the 's'. If we are describing the dinner of lots of dogs it goes after the s:
The dogs' dinner. If the plural is always a plural like children or people, we add ' s: children's stories, people's friend.

If the noun ends in 's', like James, we do not add another: James' shoes. If a plural noun ends in 's' we do not add a second: cats' whiskers. Where one thing belongs to two people, we only use the apostrophe for the second: John and Mary's mother. Otherwise, each has an apostrophe: John's and Mary's mothers.

" " **quotation marks** are used to report direct speech.
He said, "My dog is better than your cat."

' ' **single quotes**, are used for quotes within quotes and to indicate something special about a word or phrase.

Jane told me that Mary said, "My dog is better than your cat and he said 'No it isn't', and she ran away."

The 'grand prize' was a voucher for a burger.

Sometimes, individual publishers will indicate that they like quotations, song titles or other specific titles to be in single quotes. That is their style and they will ask you to follow it. Others always use single quotes for direct speech. If you are invited to follow house style, do so.

( ) **brackets or parentheses** are used to interrupt a sentence to offer an aside or add extra information. They shouldn't be used too often because they suggest that the sentence wasn't properly thought out in the first place, but can be used for emphasis, humour or clarification.

Two of the three felons went to prison. (The third was given parole).

I smiled and said I would go with them willingly (they obviously didn't know me well), and they seemed satisfied.

Romance

In genre fiction, there is a difference between a romance novel and a romantic novel. Indeed the term romantic fiction was originally coined to describe any novel; that is, a work of fiction. Now we take it specifically to mean a love story. Love stories, like the men and women they feature can come in all shapes and sizes. Historical romance: set in an earlier period (the saucier of which became known as bodice rippers, after the cumbersome undergarments that the heroine wore beneath her gowns). Georgette Heyer is often considered to be the doyenne of this genre although there are many other fine authors, but her Regency romances, full of fashion and the argot of the time, usually featuring a spirited heroine and a sardonic hero, seem to sum up this sub-genre for many. Literary Romance: in which the novels of Jane Austen and the Bronte sisters would feature. Gothic romance: in which the action takes place behind a cloak of thrilling goose-pimply mystery, normally against the backdrop of a gloomy castle and a dark secret. Again, in the twenty-first century these often include themes like vampirism and witchcraft or the supernatural. Erotic romance: in which the protagonists normally indulge in their own particular sexual fantasies and so on.

Modern publishers have a myriad of other sub-genres such as: holiday romance, doctor and nurse romance, and contemporary romance. If this genre appeals to you, it is a good idea to review the bookshelves in your local library or bookshop and sample a few of the categories to see which suits your narrative best.

Romance fiction is generally considered to be a woman's genre, but in fact, most novels have romantic interest contained within them. After all, the themes with which all fiction deals are those of human nature; jealousy and betrayal, love and hate, death and procreation, vengeance and retribution, fidelity and honour and so on. Romance merely focuses specifically on those themes within individual relationships, and creates characters to deliver the plot. At its simplest, the theme can be summarised as boy meets girl, they fall in love, there is a misunderstanding, boy loses girl, there is reconciliation, and boy and girl live happily ever after. Of course, the plot can involve multiple boys and girls and nowadays, same sex love stories are enjoying increased popularity, but whatever the gender, the formula is basically the same.

However do not let the fact that there is an identifiable formula fool you into thinking that writing romance is easy, and that it can be done successfully with tongue in cheek. Authors who enjoy writing about love as much as their readers enjoy reading about it, write the most satisfying romance. Never underestimate your reader. Your characters must be well-rounded personalities and the detail must be impeccable. If you choose historical, or medical, or any technical theme for your narrative, you must research your period very thoroughly and be especially careful not to use expressions, which would not make sense. A noted author described the dangers of having, for example, a magnetic attraction between characters, before the principle of magnetism was understood, or his heart sending the blood coursing through the hero's veins, before medical science had discovered that the heart performed this function. It goes without saying, that contemporary slang should be avoided and period slang very carefully researched. If you find sex scenes difficult to write, then an historical setting can give you an excuse not to go into too much detail. If, on the contrary you enjoy writing about sex, erotic romance is always a popular genre. It should not however be imagined that the need for good writing, careful plotting and characterisation and a strong narrative is any the less, because the reader also enjoys the erotic content. The story should be well-written first and erotic

4

second. Contemporary romance has fewer pitfalls, but in many ways the author has to work harder to take the readers out of themselves, since familiarity breeds contempt.

Research has suggested that reading romance fiction releases the same hormones in the brain as eating chocolate and as falling in love, which accounts, in part, for its popularity. Writing it can have the same effect, so there is an added bonus in all the hard work, but without the calories. It is also a subject about which we all know a great deal, so for beginners, it fulfils the criteria of writing about what we know, and it can be very therapeutic to re-write personal history in this genre, especially if the protagonists didn't live happily ever after. All is fair in love and literature.

Beginnings

1. "Watch where you are putting your feet," he snarled, as she went into the turn. A furious blush suffused her cheeks, and she was humiliated by the tears that started in her eyes. But Ella was not going to give him the satisfaction of seeing her vulnerability. "Watch where you are putting your hands!" she snapped back. He stalked haughtily from the dance floor, leaving her more crushed than ever. He was an impossible man, but a stunningly good dancer, and Ella did not want to lose him as her partner after only three classes. She had always wanted to dance the tango. Her parents, both born and brought up in Argentina, had been world champions. Somehow, she had spent her youth avoiding dancing herself. Perhaps she was afraid to compete, to intrude into the intimacy of the dance and their close, passionate marriage. It was nearly a year since the tragic plane crash that had taken their lives, and at last she had felt that she could take to the floor. She had the same long legs, tiny waist, full breasts, and supple

spine that had made her mother so mesmeric on the dance floor, and an innate sense of the true meaning of the dance, for which the judges had always lauded her father.

Carlos watched her as she stood under the mirror ball, lost and unhappy and felt a pang of remorse for his behaviour. He would try to be more patient, to find a way to help her to give her all to the dance. She was such a promising partner, and perhaps she touched his soul in a way that he was unprepared to admit, even to himself. As the music rose, he decided that she had learned the first important lesson and he relented and sauntered back to take her in his arms once again. No smile touched his lips, and the closed line of his full mouth emphasised the stubborn chin and high cheekbones. He ran his hand through his shining black hair and pulled his shoulders back in the matador's stance. He was the picture of arrogance. Suddenly something flashed in Ella's eyes and she lifted her chin defiantly. The other dancers moved to the edge of the floor as she mirrored his stance and looking straight into his eyes, laid the flat of her hand against his chest and pushed him away...

2. Okay, so he had not told her the whole truth, he was not actually head of an award-winning advertising agency, but he could just tell, as he bought this creamy-skinned, tawny beauty a drink at the bar, that 'dentist' wasn't going to cut it. She had crossed her apparently endless legs and flashed him a smile that he would have been proud to have helped create. She ran a red-tipped finger up the frosted glass of her indescribable drink and leaned a little towards him. "That's fantastic," she said, "I'm a model, and I am so looking for a mentor to help me break into the big time." She could, he thought, be the new face of Calvin Klein or Estee Lauder, or anyone, she was so incredibly beautiful. She wriggled a little with delight. "Can you really make that happen?" she whispered, in a low, sultry voice. My God, had he said

that out loud? Did he even know anyone in advertising? Jake frantically searched his mental Rolodex, visualising it sitting neatly next to the sterilizer, back at the office. Desperately, he wondered if he could yet win her with a ride in his state of the art dentist's chair and a swill of mouthwash? After all he was a good-looking guy; tall and dark with the natural build of an athlete, rather than 'workout muscles'. He was fun to be with, well educated and getting richer every day, but would that be enough? He couldn't risk it. Suddenly, he saw it, neatly typed on the card, Jake Monroe, Hanover, Ingoldby, Frantz: Advertising Executive. His patient even had the same first name. This was only semi-identity theft. She moved almost imperceptibly closer and her expensive scent washed over him. She'd make a great dental nurse, he thought, there would be no need for an anaesthetic. He pulled himself together, as she tossed the silky mane back over her shoulder and held an olive to her full, lip-glossed lips. My God, she was incredible, he couldn't let this moment slip away. "I'll see what I can do," he said confidently, and she wrote her number on the matchbook and tucked it into his breast pocket…

3. The moon was ghostly above the skeleton of the dark trees, as the coach and pair rounded the sharp bend at breakneck speed, almost spilling them out. Surely the coachman was driving the bays too hard? Virginia's heart beat a little faster as she pulled her thin wrap about her slender white shoulders. The emerald at her throat, a gift from her fiancé, felt cold and hard against her soft, white skin. The coach pitched again and she feared that her box would be lost on the road and with it, her carefully chosen trousseau. She and her sisters had spent many hours sewing by the light of tallow candles, the exquisite silks and taffetas that Mama had scrimped and saved to purchase. Her bonnets had been re-trimmed to pass as the latest fashion and the whole lovingly packed in muslin, and lavender sprinkled between the

folds. She thought wistfully of her little brother carefully picking the blue flowers and tying them to dry in the warm kitchen. The air had been sweetly scented as the flowers gave up their essential oil and the aroma mingled with that of the fresh, rough bread that was all they could afford; set to prove upon the hearth.

She was brought rudely back into the present as the coach took another bend and the wheel left the rough track. Surely her cousin Casper would be angry if his reckless coachman lost her wardrobe and injured his treasured matched pair of bays at the same time. At sixteen, Virginia had yet to experience love, but Lord Casper's dark, brooding eyes had made her heart race, when papa had told her of the advantageous marriage that he had arranged. It was true his lordship must be twice her age, but that need be no bar to happiness, after all papa was much older than mama, and they had been the perfect model of conjugal felicity, despite the want of fortune. Lord Casper's wealth was famous, as was the gambling, carousing and wickedness of his youth, though Virginia had told herself, with a tilt of her little dimpled chin, that these stories were just jealous gossip. Strange to tell, no one in Casper's wide acquaintance in town had been able to describe Cragairn castle, wherein her betrothed now drained his cup of claret and impatiently awaited the arrival of his young and innocent bride…

4. Dad was just so embarrassing tonight. No one else's dad insists on driving his daughter to parties AND picking her up. When Floyd turned on the lights and said in his most mocking voice, "Anna Jansen, your father's here." I could have died.

He might as well have come out in his pyjamas; he looked so uncool (Dad, not Floyd, he is just amazingly cool) with his hair all stuck up on end and his sweatshirt over his shirt and tie. It even has a hood! He looked like, half asleep All the way home, Dad kept asking if I'd had a nice time, and what did I eat and stuff, as if I'd been to a

kid's birthday party, like I was five or something. Just said "Whatever".
I know it drives him mad. Texted Sara (or Zarah as she now calls
herself), to find out if Floyd had got off with anyone else after I left.
She didn't answer, which probably means she got off with him. Her
mum doesn't make her leave parties just at they are getting hot. I so
hate her. (Mum that is, not Zarah, although I don't know!) Got home
and Mum kept sniffing me for like booze or fags or something. If Floyd
walked Zarah home, and he probably did, cos they like live almost next
door to each other, she will definitely kiss him. She knows I really love
him, but I know I can't trust her and she has kissed like dozens of guys.
All the boys like her; I suppose I am lucky she lets me tag along with
her. But no one really notices me next to her. She doesn't love Floyd
like I do. I thought Floyd was going to snog me at the party, even
though I have zit on my chin, that I tried to cover with Zarah's
concealer, and then the doorbell rang. Why couldn't Dad just have
waited round the corner and like texted me to say he was there. I've
shown him how to do it and everything. I don't know if he really likes
me (Floyd not Dad, Dad says he only makes me leave and stuff because
he loves me.) Floyd always kisses someone at parties. Zarah said she
would do it with him if he asks her. I will probably die a virgin. I HATE
my life…

5. She sat at the table, scanning the wanted ads in the open
newspaper: 'Relief milker wanted, no previous experience needed',
'Kind compassionate carer to house sit, must love crocodiles', 'Chief
Executive, Pharmaceutical Company', 'Chorus girl', 'Night
watchman', 'Dog walker', 'Sausage-maker'. Who, she wondered woke
up one morning and thought to themselves, there must be a job for my
special skills, where I can really use my love of crocodiles? This was
hopeless; she really didn't know what she wanted to do, only that she
hated what she was doing now.

Emma had drifted into this job as a government clerk, because that was what was expected of her. It was safe and secure with good, if slow prospects for promotion, a solid pension, assisted mortgage etc, etc. - perfect - perfectly dull. She let her eyes slide over to the personal ads. 'Tall, dark and handsome male, gsoh, own income, seeks gorgeous, fun-loving female, 20-25, must like reptiles, for wild nights.' Reptiles? She wondered if Mr T, D and H had also placed the house-sitting ad, hedging his bets.

Still, so far, no previously undetected Mr Right had bumped into her one morning, spilling her coffee and then as he tried in vain to brush away the spill from her blouse, with a spotless white handkerchief, meeting her eyes, and realising that she was not just another girl in the office. She was beautiful and talented and desirable. Some chance in pod world! The nearest she had come to romance was an embarrassing slow dance with Patrick from accounts, at the office Christmas party, and a near miss as they shuffled tipsily by the open door of the stationery cupboard.

As a child she had craved excitement and adventure, she was known as the brave and fearless one. How had she ended up chained to a pc all day long, peopling her day dreams with characters out of a Doris Day movie, with no escape for the foreseeable future? Her eyes roamed the columns idly and there it was: 'Do you crave excitement and adventure? Are you known as the brave and fearless one? Box no 30782'...

Endings

1. The dressmaker tutted grumpily, as she stuck yet another pin into the yards of frothy tulle that enveloped Daisy from head to toe.

Daisy tried not to squeal as one of the pins found its way into the slight roll of flesh at her waist. Why had this terrible woman been chosen to fashion this dream wedding gown and transform her from tomboy to princess with the flash of a scissor blade and the whirr of a sewing machine. Let's face it, Daisy thought as she peeped into the pier glass and tried not to feel disappointed, she was never going to make the cover of Bride of the Month. Zane snapped away in the corner and fiddled with lights and lenses. Miranda had made it perfectly clear that this was her last chance to make her mark at the magazine. She had set herself up to fail again.

In the past six months, since she had been promoted to features editor, she had tried to pull bridal rabbits out of top hats and none of them had quite come off. May's feature of a dream, luxury, cruise liner wedding, following a shipboard romance, had been more like a burial at sea. June's marquee wedding for the bride and groom with the most romantic below stairs love story had looked more under the stairs than below. Miranda was losing faith in her creative ability and frankly so was she. Before she had taken this job, her life had been one long dream romance; she had a perfect relationship with Toby and the greatest apartment on the Upper East Side. Her journalistic career was proceeding nicely along the path to a Pulitzer Prize and she thought she had it all. She mustn't think about Toby, not now. He was gone and she was here, trying to change her life and shake off the past. The stylist put the veil over her newly coiffed hair and Daisy's eyes filled with tears. She didn't notice Zane's camera had stopped, as she sat down on the floor and surrounded by the tulle, put her head in her hands and wept. She didn't notice the others leaving either. How could she have been such a fool? "How indeed?" a voice echoed her thoughts. "Darling, don't cry", Toby whispered, as he pulled her to her feet and into his arms. "Marry me please, now, today, even in that terrible frock, I love you so much."

2. The castle walls seemed to close in on her as she held up her skirts and ran pell-mell up the spiral staircase towards the tower. She knew that it was a mistake, even as she ran, her heart pounding in her breast. There was nowhere for her to go, except to that terrible turret at the very top and it was impossible that she could reach even that dreadful haven, and fasten and bolt the heavy oak door behind her, before he caught her. Even now she could hear his footsteps, almost feel his breath on her neck as he pulled her against him. She shuddered at the thought of his hand at the soft skin of her throat, and his voice caressing her skin with wicked, wicked words. The candle flickered in her hand as she passed the casement, blown open by the raging storm. Surely, God in his heaven couldn't be so cruel as to rob her of the comfort of even this feeble light. What would become of her, if she succumbed to the lustful embrace of Lord Trethermere? She would be lost to decent society forever and once dishonoured, he would soon tire of her. She wept at the thought that she would never again sit at the knee of her gentle mother or look into the laughing blue eyes of her dear cousin Oliver.

If only he had come to the ball that night, as he had promised, if only she had not been so headstrong as to leave alone, taking the carriage that her host had it seemed so graciously offered. The footsteps were getting closer now, and she reached out to steady herself against the clammy stone wall of the tower. Her hand touched something soft and heavy in the darkness. She pulled back her hand sharply, then tentatively reached out again. Dear God, it was velvet, a thick curtain covering an alcove in the tower wall. She slipped behind it, and blowing out the candle flame, she held her breath.

In the silence she could hear the footsteps and their echo, though surely that echo came too soon after the first. Yes, it was another's footfall, following the slow, menacing tread of the evil Lord Trethermere. The steps were followed by a thud and the sound of something heavy tumbling against the rough stone of the steps.

Amelia dared not look out, she pressed herself against the cold stone, as this perhaps second pursuer came towards her last refuge, and a hand slowly drew back the velvet drape. As she swooned into his arms in abject terror, she dreamed she heard a familiar and oh so welcome voice, "You are safe now my darling Amelia," it's Oliver.

3. James couldn't believe that he could feel this deliriously happy. He threw back the duvet and drew back the curtains, as the glorious sunshine of a May morning filtered through new leaves of the poplar trees and danced over the waxed warmth of the wooden floor. Everything was perfect, and the nightmare of the past six months was over. In a few short hours, he would be boarding the flight for New Orleans and the new life of which he had always dreamed. His suitcase was packed and the remaining items lay on the ottoman at the foot of his bed, together with the tickets and his passport. The rest of his belongings were crated up and already shipped to the beautiful waterside house in his adopted country. After all, the visa had proved easy to acquire, and the US seemed to be ready to welcome him, as it had to so many others before.

He moved to the bathroom and turned on the shower, testing its scalding water before he stepped inside. He reached for the shower gel and lathered the suds to a rich cream, enjoying the feel of the scented balm on his skin. He turned the shower to cold and felt invigorated as the icy jets ran over his broad chest and torso. He reached out for the soft bath towel, and wrapping it around his waist, moved to the basin to shave. He swiped at the steamy glass as he lathered his face. The blade moved easily over his beard and he splashed his face with more icy water. He brushed his teeth vigorously and gargled with the minty mouthwash to which he was mildly addicted. Rubbing his thick blonde curls with another towel, he moved to the kitchen, where the coffee was almost ready. He picked up the newspaper and glanced at the headlines: war and mayhem, as usual, discontent and misery. He threw the paper down and moved back into the bedroom to dress carefully. He poured his coffee and slipped his washing gear into the suitcase and zipped it up. Taking a long last look out of the window at the park beyond, he had a moment's regret when he realised that this would be the last morning that he would look out on this idyllic scene. He washed the coffee cup carefully, and put on his jacket.

He locked the door and dropped the keys into the mailbox as he ran lightly down the stairs to the waiting car. He was free at last, free to be with the only one he had ever really loved, waiting now in the back seat of the car, as ready as he was to take a leap of faith into the unknown future, together.

4. Mr Carstairs, consultant neurologist, shook hands firmly with the young surgeon as he congratulated him. "Well done, Doctor Matthews, the operation was a complete success." "Thank you Sir", said Casper Matthews, pulling down the surgical mask and reaching behind to undo the ties of his scrubs. He was delighted to receive the older man's praise, but he didn't linger to discuss the case, he must catch up with Nurse Jameson, Natalie, before she walked out of the hospital and out of his life forever. He had been such a fool, a jealous, childish fool. She had been so patient while he finished his internship, supporting him through the long, long hours and working all the hours God sends too, to keep them afloat financially. How could he have imagined that she would ever cheat on him, with that idiot Moss, when she had assured

ROMANCE

him time and time again, with the softest of kisses, after their most passionate lovemaking, that she loved only him.

A big teaching hospital like this was a rumour-mill, a cauldron of slowly melting gossip and intrigue. Casper knew this, he had after all contributed to it often enough. What ambitious young doctor hadn't? The gallows humour that kept them sane amongst the exhaustion and disease could often trip over into something bordering on malice. Natalie had been like a breath of fresh air in the corridors of Bedchester General, with her calm, open nature, her gentle certainty. She was that rare thing, a beautiful woman who had not been ruined by her looks and the effect they had on men. Casper couldn't help but see the admiring, sometimes lustful glances that staff and patients alike gave to the ravishing, petite blonde nurse as she went about her duties. He was a man after all, and he knew what they were thinking. But it had taken him until now, and the events of this very day, to realise that Natalie was oblivious to the lewd remarks and lascivious looks of every man she passed. She simply did not notice. She was the most unself-conscious and least vain woman that Casper had ever met. He just couldn't believe that she was never tempted to swap the tired, rugged but not exactly handsome young surgeon for a better model. But Natalie could not bear to be suspected of the things of which he accused her and had, with terrible sadness, given him her ultimatum. Trust me, or I walk away forever. He had not been sure that he could do it, but now he was, and he couldn't wait to find her and tell that everything was all right; they could be married now, this week, if she liked. He pushed open the swing doors, in time to see her signing out at the nurses' station. He ran towards her, and caught her sleeve. But what if she wouldn't have him, after all he had put them through. She turned at once and her smiling eyes looked up and into his. "Congratulations, Doctor Matthews, she said with a laugh in her voice, "the operation is a complete success," and she reached up to kiss him gently on the lips.

5. I hadn't really enjoyed the hen night. This was my first, and I'd hoped my last. Still and all, I wouldn't have missed Gemma's big night for the world. Who would have thought that Gemma would be the first to get married? She may have been first to leave school (at sixteen) and first to have a baby (at sixteen and three-quarters) but first to walk up the aisle, or rather across the grass to the goalmouth at the park where First Division, Bedchester Rovers play their home matches, I don't think so. So Gemma had finally found her Mr Right, and guess what, he also turned out to be Cameron's dad, so at last they would be a real family. I always thought it was someone else who was Cam's dad. But it seems Gem was seeing her footballer on the sly. Not that he was more than an apprentice then.

I couldn't be happier for her. I love that girl, stupid cow though she is sometimes. I dressed up in a stupid tee shirt and put on a kiss-me-quick stetson and we hit the Comedy Store, the six of us, all from Motley Comprehensive, class of 2000; the Millennium babes. We drank Tequila slammers and made stupid prats of ourselves, but Gemma had a good time, and that's what matters. She deserves it you know. Bringing up young Cam, on her own, working in the travel agent and studying for her A levels at night. Mr Right says he'll support her through university. He bloody, better had too. She's a good girl Gemma, and it's about time she got a break.

I didn't really want to be a bridesmaid either, to tell you the truth, all those wags and models and shiny cars; it's not really my thing. Not really Gemma's either, I'd have thought, but OK magazine paid a packet for the pictures, so there you go. Gem had a beautiful dress; she really looked like a million dollars. I got a pretty gorgeous dress too, and I didn't scrub up too badly when it came to it. Gem said to use plenty of blusher, cos I was a bit pasty from all that studying at University. I must have looked okay anyway, because the best man, seemed to take a shine to me, and if truth be told, I'd always fancied

him. I hadn't seen him since I broke up with him, and broke my heart, when we were in the lower sixth. I've dusted off the old Stetson and Gem's had some classy T-shirts printed. We're off down the Comedy Store tonight, for a few laughs before I walk up the aisle next week. Who'd have thought it eh?

(H) = Historical   (M) = Modern

Adventurer (H)	hero (Male version of gold-digger)
Adventuress (H)	a gold digger
Advertising	
Executive (M)	hero
Airline Pilot (M)	hero
Alluring (H)(M)	attractive
Amorous (H)(M)	loving
Ardent (H)(M)	truly, madly, deeply
Aristocrat (H)(M)	hero
Attraction	
Ball (H)	venue for romance
Barouche (H)	kind of horse-drawn coach
Bawdy (H)	lewd and common
Be introduced (H)	meet
Be presented (H)	meet
Beautiful	
Become acquainted (H)	meet
Billet-doux (H)	note, usually love note
Bodice (H)	upper part of a dress or gown
Bosom	breasts
Bounder (H)	a love rat, not to be trusted
By chance (H)(M)	way of meeting
Cad	not quite as bad as a bounder
Carnal (H)(M)	of the body, usually lustful
Castle (H)	venue for meeting
Charmer (H)(M)	male or female
Charming (H)(M)	characteristic of charmer

Club/bar (M)	venue for meeting
Country House (H)	venue for meeting
Dance (H)	less grand than a ball
Dating agency (M)	way of meeting
Doctor (H)(M)	potential hero
Doting/ Lovesick (H)	descriptions of love
Enamoured (H)	very keen on
Enchanting (H)	description, usually of heroine
Enticing (H)	description, usually of heroine
Entrancing (H)	description usually of heroine
Erotic (M)	usually sexual love
Fake rake (H)	(someone thought to be bad who turns out to be good)
Fascinating (H)	very attractive, with an air of mystery
Fascinator (H)	as above
Fervent (H)	rather feverish love
Fireman (M)	hero
Fond (H)(M)	not very passionate affection
Fortune-hunter (H)	cad after the heroine's money
Glamorous (M)	artificially beautiful and sexy
Handsome (H)(M)	good looking
Helena (H)	heroine name
Highstepping pair (H)	thoroughbred horses
Holiday (M)	possible venue for meeting
Hunk (M)	not clever, but irresistibly attractive
Hunters (H)	horses for fox hunting

Indifferent (H)(M)	not interested
Infatuated (H)(M)	obsessed, but not in love
Inn (H)	pub with rooms
Internet (M)	world wide web, possible meeting place
Island (H/M)	possible meeting place
Lace (H)(M)	fabric, expensive and feminine
Languish (H)(M)	to be so in love that he or she moons about over love-object
Lascivious (H)(M)	sexually predatory
Lavinia (H)	heroine name
Lecher (H)(M)	sexually predatory
Letter (H)(M)	useful plot device and means of communicating
Lovesick (H)(M)	unable to do anything but think of loved one
Madcap (H)	impetuous
Mansion (H)	possible meeting place, usually sinister
Matched pair (H)	carriage horses
Maudlin (H)(M)	mawkishly miserable
Misunderstood	bad boy, pretending to be good
Muslin (H)(M)	light semi-transparent dress fabric
Mysterious stranger (H)(M)	hero in disguise or a man who is after the heroine's virtue
Party (M)	possible meeting place
Personal Ads (M)	possible meeting place
Poor man (H)	but secretly of noble birth

Post chaise (H)   public stagecoach

Rake (H)   probably a gambler and a drunkard, not to be trusted

Rapturous (H)   deliriously happy

Roderick (H)   hero name

Rogue (H)   loveable, bad boy who can be redeemed

Rugged (H)   craggy, strong, often describes heroes

Seductive (H)(M)   alluring, tempting

Sensual (H)(M)   appealing to the senses

Sexy (M)

Silk (H)(M)   luxury, fine, smooth fabric

Stockings

Tender (H)(M)   loving and gentle

Tendresse (H)(M)   a fondness

Villain (H)   wicked man

Voluptuous (H)(M)   curvy

Voyage (H)(M)   journey both real and metaphorical

Whimsical (H)(M)   light-hearted, fey, impetuous

Wild (H)(M)   untamed

Winsome (H)(M)   appealing

SCIENCE FICTION

Science Fiction, like each genre in this book really cannot be bluffed and it is certainly the most difficult to fudge. It does contain some of the most imaginative and moving stories in print, but if you feel you would like to try your hand at it, it is really important to do proper and detailed research. Science Fiction aficionados are very on the ball and quick to spot and expose a bluffer. One of the appeals to the reader of this type of book is the hardware, the technical language - the very geekiness of it.

Traditionally, it is a genre that appeals more to men than women, but sales figures do not necessarily bear this out. Perhaps it is because in the late twentieth and early 21st century, these novels have contained within them subjects such as war and politics, technology and metaphysics. These are of course, by no means exclusively male interests, heaven forefend, but sci-fi has replaced to a degree the fiction of war that was a peculiarly male preserve. It has also stolen readers from the very popular Western, as an exploration of man the pioneer versus unyielding nature, discovering and facing the unknown at both the physical frontiers and the frontiers of knowledge. Readers understand both the science part and the fiction part, and it is important that the writer understands it too. Don't be discouraged, it is possible to gain enough of a basic understanding of astronomy, nuclear physics, quantum mechanics, rocket science and even genetic engineering and medicine to extrapolate a theory of your own. Start with quite simple definitions of terms from an encyclopaedia and a dictionary. Educational books aimed at quite young children also give sensible information on these hugely complex subjects.

As with much 21st Century genre fiction there is a degree of crossover, especially between science fiction and fantasy. It is however generally accepted that science fiction takes place within the possible application of science, as it is known, or the logical hypothetical extension of it, rather than an unbridled fantasy version. The hypothetical extensions may be improbable, but they could be, at least theoretically, possible. Science fiction is also by consensus, expected to take place in the past or a near-ish future, but not in the present. Fantasy may contain elements of Science Fiction, but it is not bound by such conventions. Early Sci Fi did not apparently contain much sex or swearing, although that is no longer the case. However, there was something compelling about the undercurrents of sex that ran underneath the Lycra or its equivalent in the early examples.

Interestingly, science fiction writers have often been attracted to using this medium to explore moral and ethical dilemmas facing contemporary society, and examine how human beings might respond to them, as well as by the hardware and terminology of science. There is some debate about which can be classed as the first science fiction novel, though many consider it to be Mary Shelley's *Frankenstein* and most of us are familiar with H.G. Wells' *War of the Worlds*. The huge popularity of Sci-Fi in the late nineteen forties, fifties and early sixties, especially in the cinema, tended to reflect the concerns of a world, which had just made staggering scientific breakthroughs in the shadow of the Second World War, such as splitting the atom and creating the 'H' bomb and the 'A' bomb, which could wipe out the world. At the same time, medicine was making extraordinary leaps forward and the race to explore space had begun. It was very much in the public consciousness that these discoveries could have horrendous applications for mankind, as well as beneficial ones. People were afraid of what lay behind the doors science could open and worried, quite rightly, about whether human beings were morally equipped to deal with the power it offered. They were also pre-occupied by the threat of outsiders to their way of life. Aliens never did come to borrow a cup of sugar, or out of curiosity and they must always be defeated to save the world. World war will create that kind of fear. The sense of anxiety was exacerbated by the Cold War and the accompanying angst that either the Americans or the Russians would secretly gain the upper hand in the development of science, and use their power to force their ideologies onto one another and the rest of the world.

It would be useful to look at the kinds of topics that exercise us now in the scientific field, when looking for inspiration for your own work. Newspapers are full of scientific stories. Some make it to the front page, like global warming, cloning, organ transplants and genetic modification. Others remain in the science pages and these can yield gems for the budding Sci-Fi writer. Literature and science also have links, which might not be instantly obvious. In the first place, it is often in developing technology and science that language develops. Scientists are always looking for words, which describe and define their work objectively and concisely, and when they can't find them, they invent them, and new technologies and discoveries give us new words. Look at the rich vocabulary that computer science has added to our language, in our own time. Words themselves can be an inspiration. Go to a local or national science fairs for ideas too, read about new building materials and techniques as well as drug breakthroughs and rocket science. An idea for a story often begins with 'What if?'

The following beginnings and endings and indeed the buzzwords list are just here to inspire you, and are by no means comprehensive, so don't be put off by the terminology. As always, fiction tends to deal with universal themes; love and hate, birth and death, survival, pain and suffering, joy and pleasure, jealousy and power. Provided that you are comfortable with the vocabulary and spacescape available to you in Science Fiction, any plotline and characters can exist within it. It can also be extremely liberating in a creative sense to be constrained by the 'rules' of a genre. Remember, science may have split the atom but science fiction split the infinitive and made it acceptable 'to boldly go'.

BEGINNINGS

1. His breath was ragged now as he powered up the incline. Nothing in the training manual had prepared him for this. The months at boot camp seemed like a picnic compared with the past week. The leaders were far ahead of him now, while the losers were so far behind that he could imagine himself to be totally alone. He paused to catch his breath and drink a little of his precious water. He knew he should conserve it, and who knew when he would find a fresh supply, in this perpetual darkness. If only he had not dropped the light map he might have a chance. As it was he had relied upon what the mentors had described as instinct. This power had not been used in living memory and he had worked hard to develop a rudimentary skill in auditory noticing. Visual identing would not be much help to him in the thickness of the dark, but the lingual bud teasing and nasal recognition had saved him from poisoning when his feeder tube had ruptured and he had been forced to forage for nourishment.

Now he tried to recall the fifth lesson, extended digital exploration. His digits were frail, but the exercises were beginning to pay off and using them to 'feel' his way along the precipitous path might be his only hope of survival. He tried breathing again, and this time the air seemed to fill his tiny lungs with oxygen. He was even beginning to imagine a landscape beyond the sharpness of his world. Perhaps that landscape would be many-hued but how would he distinguish between the shades? How would he know what to call them without a companion with whom to share the naming? He began to whimper as he contemplated the rest of his journey without another living presence to accompany him…

2. It was hours since they had passed through the asteroid storm, not that time means much out here; Day, night, weight - all meaningless. Space was an insomniac, anorexic's heaven, he thought to himself, and smiled. At least thinking was still possible, and smiling. Perhaps the regular crew had created routines to punctuate their time; clean teeth, exercise, have a cup of coffee, and call it morning. Or maybe they made crosses on the wall like a cartoon prisoner in a dungeon, to mark the passing of time. Teams of psychologists had undoubtedly studied and analyzed each member's personality and found ways to make each feel secure, and not disoriented by the endless sameness of the hours. Of course, they all had specific tasks too. Engineering, communications, catering even, had to make constant checks, and perhaps repairs, to the craft and the equipment to maintain the flight, and guarantee their safe return to earth. Sadly, he had missed being profiled. He had learned about the responsibilities from his library of sci-fi DVDs and novels. How long had they been in space? He had no idea and began to feel anxious. If the crew were constantly checking every part of the spacecraft why had no one found him yet? Maybe they were not as conscientious as they should be? Maybe they were all dead? Perhaps, this one corner of cargo bay seven was the only place that the plague, which had infiltrated the craft, had not reached? Maybe, there was no one here with him, spinning through space and time, no one human that is? Perhaps stowing away on Icarus 1V's flight to Jupiter had not been a good idea...

3. Thomas did not perspire; His face was never suffused with a blush of exertion or embarrassment. His pulse was barely discernable at the monthly check-up required by his 'employers'. Nothing ruffled his pale, corn-coloured hair, greying now at the temples. No expression on his clean-cut handsome face revealed his thoughts or feelings. Nothing marred the perfect line of his Armani suit. No scuff or speck of dust touched his highly polished Italian shoes. His perfectly knotted burgundy tie met the sharp angles of his spotless white shirt collar at a precise angle. The smile he now directed at the clerk behind the airline desk didn't disturb the steeliness of his grey eyes with any touch of warmth or humour. The man shifted uncomfortably in his swivel chair and adjusted his own professional manner. Thomas inclined his six-foot frame imperceptibly towards the clerk. He did not bother to frame the question, but slightly raised a quizzical eyebrow as he presented his documents. The clerk began to punch information into his computer, feeling unaccountably intimidated by the quiet assurance of the man that seemed to say 'Just give me the solution to this problem; no excuses, no explanations; just the new flight details and the upgrade to first class that is my due.' and all without uttering a word. The clerk began to sweat, as the screen failed to provide the instant response this man would undoubtedly require. The noisy family, anxious to be on their way to the newly-opened 'Realityworld', fidgeted behind Thomas in the line, and intruded into his concentration. Thomas stood perfectly still and looked into the eyes of the clerk. The sweat began to cool on the man's upper lip and the hairs on the back of his neck began to rise…

4. Eight-four set his weapon to stun and waited for the doors to the cargo bay to open. He had not chased this perp across the galaxy to have him bi-locate or evaporate the moment the weapon was fired. Right now, in Earth time, NASA needed to know what he knew about the hologram chummy had stolen and who had employed him to acquire the information it contained.

Eight-Four was excited, the synapses in his cerebral circuit board were fizzing and the pseudo-adrenalin in his fibre veins was pumping: android the hunter after his prey.

Sure, the shape-shifter knew he was on his trail, but unlike Eight-four he was an organism, and organisms need time to recover from injury and exhaustion, food to sustain them, and light to process that food. Eight-four had deprived Candna of all three during the light years of his pursuit. Candna was selling to the highest bidder and NASA needed to know who, or what was turning up at the auction and why. Eight-four wondered for a moment what was so red-alert important about this hologram. After all, hadn't humankind already faced every possible threat to its continued existence and survived? Sure, the planet wasn't so blue and green anymore, but the simulacrum of life in the biospheres hadn't troubled them for light years. Some of the more sensitive souls might hold some vestigial memory of a world of air and light, but their clever bodies had adapted over the generations and most of their mental problems could be kept in check with doses of immemoex in the 'water' supply.

Eight-four slipped quietly inside the cargo bay, melding with the ivory white compound of the walls, which was the closest he could get to shape-shifting. He found himself wondering about the creature that had inspired this technology, the chameleon, a colour-changing lizard, long since extinct and yet the humans experienced them all the time in the holograms of New Earth. Eight-four felt supercharged, then a slight dip in the surge of energy dizzied his circuits. What, he wondered, was he doing wondering? He wasn't programmed to wonder. He was programmed to synthesise emotion; he was programmed to anticipate and to empathise and even to weep if weeping was called for, but he wasn't programmed to wonder. Then he glimpsed the shape-shifter directly opposite him in the cargo bay. The creature was clever; Eight-four nearly laughed out loud, as the identical Mark X android emerged from the wall and aimed his identical weapon towards him, set to stun...

5. James steered the dinghy through the green, stagnant waters and longed to lift the visor on the protective helmet that he wore. He wouldn't do it of course, or the swarms of malarial mosquitoes would cover his face in seconds. Either that, or the poisonous gases would fill his lungs and he would cease to breathe. James had seen all the safety dvds. Who could miss them, projected into the dark Suffolk sky, like vapour trails from the now redundant aircraft. 'Move to higher ground; maintain your inflatable foundations', they exhorted. What did they think he was doing, out here, in the last light of a darkening sun, sweltering in the protective suit, fishing for salmon? He checked and rechecked the huge inflatables on which his family 'home' was constructed. Like checking an old-fashioned bicycle tyre for punctures, he mused, not for the first time! He looked for tiny, telltale bubbles and marked any thinning areas with chalk. Surely, by now the boffins could have come up with another way to do this - a better way? It had been fifty years since the effects of climate change (climate change his grandparents had so resolutely ignored, he reminded himself bitterly), had been seen in the rising water table. They had called it flash floods and blamed La Nina or El Nino (the little Spanish boys and girls for pity's sake?) and carried on regardless, spewing carbon dioxide out into the atmosphere. They had put all their faith in science and none in nature, and now James' generation lived in the consequences of the experience that had triumphed over hope. At least Cassy would be waiting for him when he had moored the boat and had negotiated the decontamination chamber. They had received the procreation permission at last and he was eager to set about the process of trying to produce the one child per unit permitted. Thank God, the fertility police had not uncovered his previous indiscretion. Somewhere on this God-forsaken planet there was a child bearing his DNA, and Cassy was desperate to beat her biological clock...

ENDINGS

1. As the spacecraft spun inexorably towards the black hole, the crew knew that this would be their final mission. They would never return to Earthbase 5, at least not in this lifetime. Jemo the most advanced android that had ever been developed wondered if he should simulate some emotion, to 'fit-in' with the rest of the crew. But this crew, under the iron rule of Captain Augustus seemed unable to express their own human emotions, now that they were faced with the ultimate crisis.

The atmosphere on the bridge was both electric and deadly calm. The navigation officer diligently pressed his plasma screen, and gazed upward, as did they all, into the nothingness of space. No one spoke, although the communications officer could be heard droning the same, age-old message, over and over again, into the open com. channels in the hope that some craft, somewhere, would pick up their signal. 'Mayday, Mayday, HMS Icarus, star system Neptune, Mayday, Mayday.' Every so often, she would pause and the entire bridge would strain to hear some response from another craft, however alien.

It was impossible to calculate the time left before Icarus disappeared forever. It was impossible to imagine what lay within the black hole ahead. All that they could do was their jobs, efficiently and methodically. Would they halt, Jemo wondered, to say a fond goodbye to one another, to exchange a few words of love and regret. Not this crew, on this mission. Earthbase 5 would consider the mission a success, whether they returned or not. They had intercepted the weaponry aboard the pirate craft, bound for the rebels on Solarbase 7.

They had averted a solar disaster by their brave actions. Indeed, the captain could almost believe that Earthbase 5 would be relieved at this particular outcome. The most advanced weapons ever created, and the most destructive, would disappear with them, forever. In the final analysis this would be safer for the universe than re-entering the earth's atmosphere with them on board and then having to find a safe method of disposal. As the systems failed simultaneously, with every man and woman at his post, Jemo felt certain that this was the safe method of disposal that the commander-in-chief had planned all along. And then – nothingness.

2. The animals moved restlessly in the cages, affected by the gathering storm. The keeper moved amongst them crooning a soft lullaby, the words of which had long since been forgotten. At the sound of his voice, the bigger creatures calmed and settled amongst the faux straw that served as bedding.

The little ones, the rodents and smaller mammals, skittered nervously against the bars, but made no other sound. The bird's wings, cruelly clipped, fluttered uselessly against the netting of the aviary. The biggest and fiercest animals would have to wait for their supper tonight. He would not risk being crushed or mauled as he moved between them, when the weather was so wild. At least they could no longer eat each other. He had been sorry to lose the gazelles, but lions must eat. Thankfully, he had already taken the DNA samples and Mrs. N. had begun the cloning at once. It would be nice to have the young about again. They restored your faith in any kind of a future.

The ark, rocked gently as the swell increased and the wind turned to the North East. Noah continued his rounds, pouring water into the bowls and pellets into the troughs. Funny, how the animals liked their food to look like food, the taste seemed less important, which was just as well, since nearly all the foodstuffs were made from recycled paper, stored a hundred years ago, for some unknown purpose. Noah fashioned the mulch into haunches of meat and tiny creatures for the carnivores, and leaf-like meals, copied from the holograms of ancient times, for the herbivores. Below, he could hear Mrs. N. battening down the hatches, and screwing down everything that could be damaged when the waves really began to rise. There was no shortage of oceans and seas for Noah to sail since the polar ice caps had melted, but the charts from the 21st Century were rendered useless in the ever-changing seascape. Sometimes they had the excitement of discovering a new creature, one that had adapted to the warmer temperatures, and survived. Noah's job was to collect them, when he could, two of each kind, male and female and add them to the living cargo of the ark. There was no longer any land, and he wasn't sure why he was still following the directive, but where there's life there's hope, as Mrs. N was fond of saying, and one day the waters might recede and he and Mrs. N. would be ready to restock the world that man had so carelessly thrown away.

3. Martha placed the baby in the cradle and walked away. In her mind's eye she pictured him, pink and warm after a bath, replete with mother's milk, sleeping gently against the swell of her breast. She knew that this was wrong of her, and she had to concentrate exceptionally hard to create the mind block that would keep out the dream police. Now that the rule about thinking had been relaxed, the authority needed some new ideas it was said; she had hoped that the dream embargo would be lifted too. But Michael said that dreams were far more subversive than thoughts, and it was unlikely that they would ever again be free to live within the realm of their imaginations. Michael did not know that Martha had inherited the ability to block from her own mother, it would only make him afraid for her, and for their child. Martha was an obedient subject in all other respects. She had allowed Michael to take the infant to the crèche with the other little citizens. She gave no outward sign that she imagined another life for their fragile family, one in which they would be able to live together. She returned to the women's shed and sat at her computer as she was instructed. She computed the complex algorithms without difficulty in her head, but the authority preferred to receive their data from the computers, so she had kept this little secret to herself too. She supposed that limiting the imagination made it difficult for them to comprehend that mathematical genius and creativity were not, as they thought, mutually incompatible.

She logged out as her shift came to an end and saved the data to the main database. She washed her hands and her mind in the washroom and passed into the living quarters. Tonight was another procreation night for her sector, so their partners would be visiting. The doers were already erecting the privacy barriers. It was unlikely that she would conceive again, quite so soon after the birth of their little citizen, but it was possible. Martha ached for her baby, to hold him and love him, as she knew she should. As she prepared for Michael, she blocked the authority again and began to plan their escape. It was possible, she knew to find a corner of the universe where there was no authority, and she had plotted the route, now all she had to do was persuade Michael to steal the baby.

4. "I don't want to be in this time zone," the child whined, as his mother pulled him along by the hand. "It's dirty, and smelly, and I'm frightened." His mother was frightened too, very frightened.

This zone had not been her intended destination when they had turned the time key that morning. Jacob was doing a school project on life in the 21st Century, and good mother and former teacher that she was, she thought a quick field trip would be a good idea. However, something had evidently gone awry. She had intended for them to spend the day in around 2050, when the emissions had at last been cleared and the atmosphere was fit to breathe again. She had not expected to tip up in 2020, when the world put the chaos back into chaos theory. Jacob was right, it was dirty and smelly and frightening. The people looked so grey and miserable, an ageing population with sharp memories of the beauty that had been to haunt them, and even sharper experience of the ugliness that was. These elders were issued with little scooters and trolleys to help them get about, but they were so lonely, separated from all the promise and hope of youth. The streets smelled of the detritus of their lifetimes. They were two weak to clean it up themselves and the youth had long since moved upwind of the decaying cities.

Jacob scowled, despite his mother's admonitions, at the poor old folk who bared their gums excitedly at the sight of the mother and child. Some even muttered, "Madonna, Madonna, help us," as they passed by. They would be helped in the future, or at least their children would, when they reached the age of decay, but the mother was forbidden to tell them this, so she could not relieve their suffering. She had seen the future and it was a tribute to the adaptability and ingenuity of the species. The cities were bright and clean, the air sweet and pure and healthcare for the elders made their declining years a joy.

But not for these people, they would live amongst the gloom and squalor for the rest of their days. They would also live with the guilt and fear that this was the world that their greed and folly had created for their children to inherit. Perhaps she could just make them a feel a little better about that. As she turned the time key to take them home, she dropped a time card into the mailbox. The future is bright, her time card said, Wish you were here.

5. The planet's surface may be unattractive to the eye, and poisonous to the health, but there was no doubt that these Plutonian's really knew how to party. Captain Ahab had been trading with these little guys for ten years now, and had learned what warm and wonderful non-human-beings they were.

He guessed that living as they did in biospheres below the surface of their planet, they had evolved to live in harmony. What started out as a system of politesse and diplomacy had become a truly tolerant society, or so Mica had told him.

He was a little worried that they were vulnerable to exploitation by the waves of immigrants from throughout the universe, who had discovered only recently, that little piece of heaven that was Pluto. Ahab was thinking seriously of settling down here, marrying a nice little Plutonian chick like Mica, and making that better life for himself that was always just a few light years away.

Mica was looking at him thoughtfully. Telepathy had its drawbacks. How was she to tell this muddled human that she was happy with their relationship just the way it was. Mica had no intention of settling down with Captain Ahab, she had her eye (literally, since Plutonians had one central eye) on Moca, the young and virile Plutonian next door. She loved Ahab in her way, but not in his way, but the last thing she wanted to do was hurt his feelings. Mica decided to help him save face by giving him the opportunity to leave her. She felt that it would be best if she introduced the idea of Moca now, so that he would not see this as choice, which left him out in the cold. Mica checked her phrase book and behaviour guide; these aliens could be so sensitive. She poured them both a drink, and asked if they could talk. He knew what was on the cards then, but he let it go,

The recreational sex had been great, and apparently could continue, but she had given her hearts to another. It wasn't him it was her; they'd always be friends. Yeah, sure, he thought as he returned to his own pod. Let's just be friends.

Acceleration	speed propulsion of craft
Ageing	common theme, also way of cheating time when involved in space travel
Android	robot that looks and behaves like a human being
Asteroid	an irregularly shaped rock that orbits the sun mostly in a band asteroid belt between the orbits of Mars and Jupiter
Black hole	an object in space thought to contain a celestial object, with such a strong gravitational pull that no matter or energy can escape from it
Breathing	the action of taking in essential oxygen and pushing out carbon dioxide. To date no other planet has been found on which human beings can breathe, so breathing apparatus is needed
Celestial	relating to, involving or observed in the sky or outer space
Ceres	the largest asteroid orbiting between Mars and Saturn
Clone	a plant or animal, or other organism that is genetically identical to its parent
Comet	an astronomical object made up of ice and dust with a long luminous tail produced by vaporization when its orbit passes too close to the sun
Communication	means of transmitting information, images etc between two or more points,

	language, devices for doing so, wireless technology, web cam etc.
Cryonics	the study or practice of keeping a technically dead body at an extremely low temperature in the hope of restoring it to life later: used to transport crew, pioneers etc to distant planets during space travel to counter the effects of travelling faster than the speed of light.
Earth's core	the centre of the earth
Eris	dwarf planet
Extra terrestrial	beyond or outside the earth, used to describe creatures from other planets
Faster Than Light (FTL)	means of propulsion faster than the speed of light required for stories of star-based adventures
Flying saucer	space craft
Galactic	of the galaxy
Galaxy	a group of billions of stars and their planets, gas and dust that extends over many thousand of light years and forms a unit within the universe
Generational ship	a space station
GM	genetic modification
Gravity	the attraction that the Earth or another celestial body exerts on an object on or near its surface

Gravitational pull	the mutual force of attraction between all particles or bodies that have mass
Graviton	a hypothetical particle with zero charge and rest mass that is to be considered to be the quantum particle of the gravitational interaction
Graviton-polarity generators	reverse polarity of gravitons
Guidance systems	the means by which navigation is achieved
Hibernation biology	means by which crew etc can travel faster than the speed of light without ageing
Intergalactic	between galaxies
Jupiter	the largest planet in the solar system, fifth in order from the sun
Lift-off	the moment of launch for a spacecraft
Lunar atmosphere	the atmosphere of the moon
Mars	the third smallest planet in the solar system and the fourth planet from the sun
Matter transformer	a hypothetical way of travelling from one place to the other by dissolving and then reassembling matter
Mercury	the smallest planet in the solar system and the one nearest to the sun
Meteoroid	a mass of rock in space, often a remnant of a comet that becomes a meteor when it enters the earth's atmosphere

Moon	the earth's only natural satellite, the nearest astronomical body to the earth, any natural satellite revolving around a planet
Neutron	a neutral elementary particle of the baryon family with a zero electrical charge
Neutron star	a celestial body consisting entirely of neutrons, the remnant of a star that has collapsed under its own gravity
Orbit	the path that a celestial body such as a planet moon or satellite follows around a larger celestial body such as the sun
Paradox	a proposition or situation that seems to be absurd or contradictory, but in fact is, or could be true
Planet	an astronomical body that orbits a star, and does not shine with its own light, especially one of the nine orbiting the sun in the solar system
Pluto	the smallest planet in the solar system smallest in diameter, and on average furthest away from the sun
Pod	something in which an organism has all it needs to sustain life. e.g. pea in pod
Propulsion	the means by which things go forward, relating to space craft
Proton	a stable elementary particle that is a component of all atomic nuclei and carries a positive charge equal to that of the electron's negative charge

Quantum	the smallest discrete quantity of a physical property, e.g. electromagnetic radiation
Robot	an automaton
Saturn	the second largest planet in the solar system and the sixth planet from the sun. Saturn has bright rings made up of orbiting fragments of rock
Shuttle	something which goes backwards and forwards, usually a smaller spacecraft, which is contained within a larger
Space ark	space station
Space-time continuum	special theory of relativity relating to time travel
Space probe	a satellite or other spacecraft that is designed to explore the solar system and transmit data back to earth
Spherical thruster	means of propelling a spacecraft
Star system	see galaxy
Sun	the star at the centre of a solar system providing light and heat
Telepathy	reading of the unspoken thoughts of another
Thermal protection	protection from extremes of temperature
Thrust	movement or impetus
UFOS	unidentified flying objects
Uranus	the seventh smallest planet in the solar system and the seventh from the sun

Vaporize   to destroy someone or something so completely that he/it is turned into a gas or vapour

Velocity   a measure of the rate of change in position of something with respect to time, involving speed and direction

Venus   the fourth smallest planet in the solar system and the second planet from the sun

Warp drive/speed   imaginary means by which space craft can be propelled at many times faster than light, to avoid the difficulties associated with time dilation.

Zero gravity   where there is no gravitation between objects

WESTERN

The Western has not been conspicuous in the bestsellers list for a while, (with the possible exception of the atypical *Brokeback Mountain* by Annie Proulx), but it still has a dedicated readership amongst aficionados and in libraries. Traditionally, good versus evil was played out in the dust, with all guns blazing, and justice was meted out to gamblers, rustlers and outlaws by drunken judges and lynch mobs. The simplicity of the mid-twentieth century plots of traditional westerns, and their place in pulp fiction, has perhaps given way to more complex treatments of these same themes in thrillers and detective stories, science fiction and fantasy.

The latter two, especially, offer wide scope for imaginative exploration of human nature revealed at the extremes, whilst still exploiting the fertile ground that the colonisation of new frontiers presents, albeit in another universe, or even another dimension. Readers have, in general, become more interested in urban adventure, high technology and modern metaphor. Maybe the Western is due for a major revival? The television series 'Deadwood' has been a huge success on both sides of the Atlantic in recent years.

For some writers and many readers, there is a comforting familiarity about this genre, as experienced through cinema and television, as well as novels and comics. The pioneers of the West gave us real-life, classic heroes and villains like Jessie James, Wyatt Earp, Pat Garrett and Billy the Kid, Wild Bill Hickok, Buffalo Bill, Doc Holiday, Annie Oakley, Davy Crockett and many more. There is endless scope for representing their particular stories, and academics and historians provide more and more accurate information from research about the reality of their lives, and life on the frontier in general. The known facts about these individuals can offer a template so that the Western can also provide a place for your own characters to live, laugh, love and die, if the genre appeals to you.

Western fiction has always been rooted in historical fact, roughly covering the period between 1865 and 1890, and located in the six states from North Dakota to Texas, and tells of pioneers and gold miners, wagon trains and cattle drives, saloon bars and strong, silent heroes hunting down cold-hearted bandits.

If the setting captures your imagination, this can be a genre in which, in a less-crowded landscape, the new writer can tell his or her story just as effectively as any other. The universal themes of love and death, honour and pride, courage and cowardice, comedy and tragedy, tenacity and survival can all be set against a backdrop of gulches and tumbleweed, livery stables and gambling dens. Imagine, for example, that you want to develop a story based on a very modern theme like the experiences of an immigrant displaced by war, a stranger in a strange land making a new life, with nothing but the clothes on his or her back and a determined spirit. Many of the pioneers of the old west were immigrants, escaping the poverty and persecution of old Europe. The opening up of the territory presented opportunities for people who had little or nothing. It is as possible for you to explore the humanity, emotions and actions, triumphs and disasters of such a character in this setting as in the 21st Century world in which we live now. Human beings don't change fundamentally, even though history gives them a different theatre in which to operate.

Do not however, be tempted to write a Western with your tongue in your cheek. Just because the vocabulary of the Western seems familiar, many are tempted to pastiche. As with Romantic fiction, this approach is rarely successful. You must find the setting and the opportunities that the Western offers genuinely appealing as a vehicle for your own story, and then tell it sincerely.

Like most modern genres, there is a considerable amount of crossover in 21st Century Western fiction. If you haven't read any for a while, you may be surprised by the subtly of the plots and the degree to which the stories contain far more uncensored and explicit violence and less 'tomato ketchup' than previously. There are also fewer confrontations with 'Indians', since we have all become better educated about Native North American culture. Although, in a sense, Westerns are historical action thrillers, and the nomenclature and attitudes were normal at the time, twenty-first century writers do shy away from using unacceptable racial stereotyping to establish authenticity. Thankfully, you will therefore find fewer references to 'red skins' and 'injuns' in contemporary cowboy stories. You are more likely to find decent, complex characterisation and historically accurate detail, if Native North American protagonists feature, than in the fiction of the 1940s and 50s. There is now a greater emphasis on the accurate history and geography, weapons technology, and transportation of the period all round, and if your Western fiction is to stand up against other contemporary work, you will need to do detailed research.

Modern Westerns need more intricate plotting and characterisation (less black hat bad, white hat good) and most offer their fair share of uninhibited sex! The days of the virtuous school marm versus the easy, saloon dance hall girl with a heart of gold are deader than the gunslingers buried in the graveyard up on Boot Hill. Life on the frontier is hard and lonely and men are men and women are women and in the minority, (with the possible exception of *Brokeback Mountain* – again) and passions run high. Relationships of all kinds have to be carved out of the unyielding, natural geographical and social landscape of the 19th Century American west.

The beginnings and endings that follow offer flavour and variety, and are designed to give your imagination a start, as do the buzzwords listed at the end of the section. The right vocabulary and your own detailed and accurate research will give your story texture and context, which allows the reader to engage and identify with your characters as they tell it. As with all period drama, you should keep your plot within the bounds of historical possibility. Do not feature inventions that have not yet been made and be careful to avoid expressions that would have been unknown. By all means outline your plot and characters before you pick up someone else's work and suffer an attack of 'kleptonesia', (accidentally picking up someone else's plots and then forgetting about it) and are unduly influenced. But, if you think that Westerns are the right genre for you, read as many as you can before you start to write. Get a feel for the style and begin with some short pieces. Go West, young man, or woman!

BEGINNINGS

1. The soft grumbling of the restless steers as they moved around, steam rising from their flanks and mingling with his cold breath, just about kept Jed awake in the saddle. They had made camp for the night in the rare, grassy hollow by the banks of the river. The water was high and clear, and cold as charity, flowing fast and fresh, swelled by the mountain snows melted in the watery spring sunlight. Clancy was a fine drive boss; he knew the territory and he had kept his promise to get men and cattle to this bend in the river before the beasts lost too much condition and the cowboys lost heart, and while they could still cross the stream in safety. Another day or two and they would have had to add another week to this drive, taking the long way round, with the cattle getting thinner and the cowboys ornerier.

They had barely lost a steer on the trail. Clancy knew that a rider circling the herd at night reassured the beasts, and discouraged the rustlers, who picked off the cattle as they drew nearer to the scattered homesteads and new townships at the end of the drive. Jed figured that on starlit nights like this one, a steak dinner could seem mighty appealing to hungry men scratching a living from the soil, and some were none to particular about how their T-bone was branded.

Still and all, Jed would not be sorry to see his bed roll and wrap his blanket around him when Saul came to take over in an hour or so. Jed took out his 'makins' from his saddlebag and rolled himself a meagre smoke. It would be a few days yet till payday and he could buy more baccy at the general store. He could smell the tobacco smoke on the wind even above the ripe earthy smell of the cattle and his own unwashed body. He was looking forward to a drink and a hot bath when they hit town, and maybe a little company. Then he would take a few days out to look for Matt. This may be the town; and maybe, just maybe he would reach it before Matt was run out of it. If his brother's gambling didn't lead him into trouble his drinking would. That or a soft-skinned woman whose husband didn't take kindly to the handsome scoundrel Jed's twin had become…

2. Lee lay very still behind the big iron wheels of the mighty engine. He moved slowly, like a snake in the darkness, with his pale face to the ground. It had taken him just one beating, six months before, to learn that when the gang bosses drank whiskey all night, it was wise to be silent and invisible. For nearly a year now they had blasted and clawed their way through solid rock to bring the railroad, and with it civilization and prosperity, to this wild land. Lee, like the other Chinese in the gang was needed for his knowledge of gunpowder and dynamite, and for his tireless labour, and the bosses gave him grudging respect when they were sober.

But when they were drunk, like now, their fear and suspicion of these men from a civilization more ancient than they could imagine would come to the fore. Because the Chinese struggled with the language, some bosses made the mistake of thinking them stupid, and their pigtails and the loose trousers and tunics in which they clothed their sparse frames, made a drink-fuelled bully think them weak and effeminate. Experience would teach the smarter of the bosses of the sharp intelligence that lay behind the smiles and quiet courtesy, and the skills in unarmed combat which the gentleness of the Chinese belied. Still, this was good work and it fed his family and whilst Lee resented having to crawl through the dust and shadows to avoid notice, he had no wish to force a confrontation, which would see him without work at best, and at worst, his wife a widow.

On this job he had found an unexpected ally in Brett Faulkner. The quiet engineer valued Lee more highly than he did the burly navvies who laid the lines and was eager to learn all he could from the young Chinese man. The unlikely and mutually respectful friendship between the tall, quiet Faulkner and the slight Chinese did not escape the navvies and did nothing to add to Lee's popularity. Fair by nature, and a strong leader, Faulkner was more than a match for the muscle-bound thugs gathered round the fire. But tonight, Faulkner was in town arranging the next stage of the line and ordering supplies. Tonight, Lee would be at the mercy of men who had not been to town in months, and fired up with the drink, the boys were looking to let off a little steam…

3. It felt to Marie that she had shed her respectable, stuffy background with her corsets and petticoats, as she stood, down to her chemise now, being appraised like a prize heifer by a woman her mama would cross the street to avoid. Belle measured Marie with a practiced eye and riffled through the trunk at her feet, bringing out lengths of linen and cambric, silk and lace.

"These should set off your colouring," she told Marie. "I reckon your sewing skills, like your singing, were learned from a French governess, so I guess you should have no trouble making up the dress." Marie had the grace to blush, So, Belle had not been fooled by her attempts to hide where she had come from, yet still the older woman asked no questions.

"Remember, your job is to attract the men into the barroom, not the bedroom and to keep them here spending their pay. It amuses Jim Macready to let us perform here as long as it brings him in a dollar. If you are looking to earn a little on the side, you should leave right now, and go join the girls in the cat house by the livery stable." Marie bridled at this. Couldn't Belle see that she was not that kind of a girl? She was hungry though, and needed this job badly and she kept her mouth closed, though the colour heightened in her pale, freckled cheeks and her curious green eyes flashed.

Belle seemed to read her mind, and her sharp features were softened by a wry smile. "The men in these parts don't always recall that their mamas brought them up to be little gentleman; sometimes they see a girl through the bottom of a whiskey glass and imagine that she is theirs for the taking. I will feed you and clothe you and give you lodgings and wages besides, but you have to learn to protect yourself." She tucked a tiny, pearl-handled pistol into Marie's garter, the steel cold against her warm thigh. "You have to love this life more than you want a life of love. One day, performers will be respected and the stage will not a storefront for men who should know better, but for now, you will need to keep your wits about you." Marie glanced in the looking glass at her reflection and gasped, a tall man in a deep-blue frock coat was standing quietly by the door listening to Belle, his eyes fixed on Marie's reflection…

4. The first outraged cries of the baby, as his lungs filled with clear, cold air, pierced the darkness of the night like an arrow. The lantern, which Dulcie held high over her mama swung in the breeze and Ma Grogan wrapped the surprised infant in a clean cotton shawl and laid

him in his exhausted mother's arms. "He's to be named Cal," she whispered, "the first precious child to be born since we crossed the border into California; a new life in our new life."

The preacher was waiting outside the wagon, with his prayer book in his hand. Dressed in black, with his hooked nose and hooded eyes, he reminded Dulcie of nothing so much as the vultures that flew high above the wagon train waiting for the livestock to die of thirst or worse. Whether he was waiting to welcome the tiny babe clinging to life or to say a few last words over his mother, who seemed to be letting go of hers, was unclear. Dulcie was suddenly filled with fury. Had they survived the treacherous journey thus far for her beloved mama to be taken now, just as the end was in sight? And for what, this bawling scrap searching hungrily to suck the last life from his mother? What kind of God would leave eleven-year old Dulcie to care for Pa and the little kids and now this greedy stranger? Hot tears spilled down her cheeks and she swiped at them with the back of her hand. She must not weep now. She must be strong for Mama and find a way to help Pa keep the family together. But who would be there for her?

Ma Grogan took the baby gently from his mother and taking the lantern from Dulcie put Cal into her arms. "Go find your pa now Dulcie," she said, "and hurry, take the baby and ask the womenfolk to find him some milk, your mama needs to rest." Dulcie knew she was lying, she might just as well say "your mama needs to die". But Dulcie knew better than to argue; she climbed down from the wagon and pushed past the preacher, heedless of his solemn words and went towards the fire. Pa would be playing cards with the other settlers, hoping to win the stake money upon which they would build their golden future …

5. The Oklahoma Kid rasped the cutthroat razor across the dirty blond stubble of his beard, enjoying the sensation. He screwed up his eyes to check his progress in the tin mirror hanging from the branch of a tree. Adjusting the angle as best he could, he thought fleetingly that it was best not to dwell on trees and hanging too long. Not so much of a kid now either, he acknowledged wryly to himself: the lines at the corners of his slate-blue eyes remained etched into his prairie-tanned face, even in repose.

With a practiced hand, he manoeuvred the blade edge around the cleft in his stubborn chin and noticed too the hard lines that ran from his straight nose to his thin lips. This was no life for a man getting on in years, nowadays his back was sore after a day's hard riding and a bed roll on the ground was no match for a feather mattress. Still and all, he could outgun and outrun the punk kids looking to take down the legend that was the Oklahoma Kid, and he could outsmart the bounty hunters and lawmen and even the Pinkerton boys 'detecting' in every two-bit town he came to.

Maybe it was time to think about becoming plain Josh Banks Esq. newspaper man for keeps this time. He lifted the leather valise down from the buckboard and unrolled the smooth linen shirt and black pants within. The vest, with just a touch of fancy Mexican embroidery buttoned over the shirt, and he shrugged on the long, black coat, brushing a speck of trail dust from the lapel.

Finally, he tied the shoe string tie at his throat and pushed a snowy lawn kerchief into his breast pocket. The kerchief, like the shirt had been sewed for him by Eliza and he fancied that he could still smell her lemon cologne in the folds of the freshly-laundered linen; foolish notion after all these years. He hitched his horse, fresh and frisky to the buckboard concealed in the brush and drew it onto the trail. He hoisted in the valise, now repacked with his shaving kit and trail clothes and the Oklahoma Kid's identity and opened the plain, gold fob watch that was all he had still of his beloved father. He stroked his horse's nose and the mare nuzzled against him. It was about time to get going, news was about ready to break in Tombstone and he was about ready to be the man to break it…

ENDINGS

1. I guess it ain't so all-fired important now, Mac thought to himself as he filed away the ownership papers to his claim in the iron-bound deed box and pushed it under his bed. Not after all the sweat and blood; the men who had perished on the trek and those who had been broken by the prospecting, the booze, or the dust, or just the plain loneliness of trying to find the key to that fortune that had brought him, like so many others out west. Now that he was rich, and could go anywhere and do anything, he found that he missed the striving more than he expected. Women were drawn to him by the glint of the gold, men wanted to shake him by the hand and call themselves his friends. The judge had suggested he run for office come July, and he might just do that. Mayor MacDougall, sounded good to his ear and he might just pick him a wife from the herd of pretty women roaming around this boom town.

Some of them were halfway decent now the outlaws and gamblers had found their niche at the Silver Star. He could maybe even raise a couple of kids and build himself a fine house right here on Main Street. Who was he kidding? Money didn't buy men like him respectability, or the kind of woman who he would want to be the mother of his children. Janie would be halfway to Santa Fe by now. My how that woman could love, and she had waited all this time for him to be ready, to feel himself worthy of her love, to feel that he had made his mark in the world and could hold his head up and ask her to be his bride. Now it was too late. He turned the lamp down a little and poured himself a couple of fingers of Rye. He had lost her and now he realised that it had all been for her, the striving. He heard a carriage in the street outside and for a moment he allowed himself to hope that she had turned back, ready to give him another chance. But the rap on the door was made by a man's hand and as he opened it, he gasped. "Howdy, Mac," said a familiar voice from the darkness just outside the lamplight, "I've come for my gold."

2. Clem wasn't gong to wait much longer. He wasn't the kinda man to hang around for anyone, and he didn't much care for the way he had been bamboozled into teaming up with Clay for this job.

Still and all, the boss knew what he was doing and like he said maybe Clem was a bit stuck in his ways. Needed a bit of new blood in the outfit, the boss said. Clay dressed a little too fine to Clem's way of thinking. He was a little too fond of the ladies too, and the whiskey. Yeah, Clem mused to himself, that Clay Jansen sure wasn't going to make old bones with his carryin on and all. Little more attention to detail and a little less talk wouldn't do no harm neither. Where was that varmint, surely the boss couldn't expect him to wait around all day for the kid to show up? This was dangerous country and Clem felt kinda exposed out here on the trail, with the sun coming up fast over the gulch. His horse whinnied restlessly and Clem gentled her. He got down and put his ear to the ground; like he'd seen them Indian scouts do and listened in the morning stillness. Well I'll be danged, he said to himself, it worked; he could feel the vibrations in the dry parched earth. Horse coming, and no mistake, and about time too. Clem took out his rifle and loaded it. Sure it could be Clay, meeting up like he was supposed to, but it could be someone else, someone with a mind to take back the proceeds of the robbery that had taken place in Tombstone the day before. Clay had stayed behind to tie up the loose ends, or so he said, but Clem reckoned he had wanted to say goodbye to that pretty young Missy he'd been cosying up to. Didn't pay to get attached in their line of business, didn't pay to stay too long in one place neither. Still Clay would learn the way that Clem had had to, if he stayed alive that long.

The horse was getting nearer now, and Clem could smell its sweat on the wind. If that was Clay, he was riding that mare hard. Clem tucked himself behind a boulder and waited. The horse drew level with his hiding place and Clay swung down from the saddle and pulling his horse behind him, joined Clem behind the boulder, his six gun loaded and aimed at the trail behind him.

Clem didn't need to ask questions, the blood coming from a bullet wound in Clay's shoulder told it own tale. He realised that he was kinda fond of the young rascal after all, so it came as something of a surprise to find Clay's gun pointed at his head, and a Marshall's badge glinting from his coat in the morning sun.

3. Lily sashayed over to the bar where the Kid was calling for another drink. She picked out the bottle of the good stuff from behind the counter and put it down in front of him, with two glasses, one for her and one for him. The Kid never took his eyes off the tall stranger dealing out the cards at the poker game out back. Lily didn't think the Kid looked mad or anything, just kind of interested, she'd have said. The stranger didn't look too concerned either, calmly shuffling and dealing, but you could tell he knew the Kid was watching him. His shoulders were a little too set, his smile a little too casual. The Kid picked up the bottle and the glasses and moved towards the stranger. Lily knew better than to argue that one of those had been for her, or to mention that this was the good stuff, the stuff she kept only for him.

She moved into the shadows behind the chair the Kid pulled up at the table. The stranger tipped his hat at her and looked the Kid in the eye, cool as you like. "Hiya Kid," said the stranger, "I guess you don't remember me too well." The Kid looked puzzled, why should he remember a man he had never seen before, and yet there did seem something familiar about this tall dark stranger, but he was danged if he could place him. "Why should I remember you?" he said, slowly picking up the cards in front of him. "No reason at all" the stranger drawled, "I guess you can't recall every face you pass on the road through life." "Do I know you, padre?" the Kid asked with an edge of impatience in his voice. It was well known that the Kid didn't hold with no Bible peddling in his town, and yet the stranger didn't look much like a preacher to Lily. "I know you, son," the stranger said, "and I'd like to get to know you better if you'll let me."

"No one calls me son, padre," said the Kid, with a touch of menace in his voice now. "I know you all I want to, right now. So why don't you drink up, on the house, and move on out of town?"

The stranger stood up slowly and downed his whiskey in one. He set the glass down and picked up his hat, and made to leave the bar. Then as he passed close by the Kid, he leaned in towards him and said softly, "I know you, son, and I kinda have a right to call you that, because I'm your pa, and we are going to get to know each other a whole lot better." For a second, Lily thought the Kid was going to embrace the stranger, as he leaned closer, but then she saw the flash of the blade and heard the soft sigh as it disappeared into the stranger's heart.

4. The train sure was the way to travel these days and Marianne liked the way the guard was courteous to everyone, and she liked the fact that there were armed Pinkerton men in the baggage car, keeping watch over the safe and passengers alike.

She wiped a smut of soot from her pale cheek and straightened her bonnet. Pa may not approve of her travelling alone like this, he was old-fashioned that way, but there were plenty of ladies aboard today, and she didn't feel out of place. Nor and she hadn't been subject to unwanted attentions, slightly to her regret. The journey west had been uneventful and comfortable. She had told her pa that the railroad was the only way to travel these days and he would see for himself that she was right, when he joined the train at Sacramento. A tall, elegant lady had got on at the last stop and she was arranging herself now opposite Marianne. Marianne smiled and offered to hold her parcels while she stowed her bags overhead.

The lady seemed very grateful, and smiled graciously and she certainly had no trouble reaching up and hefting her baggage in the rack above. My, she was strong, thought Marianne. Presently, she decided to take a turn down the train to stretch her legs, and she couldn't help noticing that the lady had pretty big feet too. When, Marianne returned, she was surprised to find her travelling companion had nodded off and was snoring in a very unladylike manner. Marianne climbed into her seat, and decided that if she had fallen asleep on the train, with her mouth wide open, she hoped some kindly stranger would wake her. The lady started awake and gripped Marianne's wrist, quite hard, where she had only gently shaken the lady's sleeve. For a moment, the grey eyes had looked slightly afraid. Marianne extricated herself from the lady's grip and explained why she had been so presumptuous as to wake her. The lady smiled her thanks and nodded understanding.

Marianne was beginning to think that there was something pretty strange about her companion when she felt the barrel of a six gun pointed at her side. "Don't say a word" the lady whispered, "just come with me." Marianne was bustled along the train to the baggage car, where the lady pushed her behind him (for Marianne realised he was in disguise) just as the Pinkerton men came blasting their way out of the car. The stranger lay dead in a pool of blood and Marianne never even knew his name.

5. Dear Mama,

The rodeo is just about ready to start and I am itching to show Miss Esme just how great a wrangler I am. The town has really begun to settle down now, since the railroad has come through. Sure it caused some local difficulty. Bad men, doing crooked deals, like shadows and isolation in which to operate, but the railroad is bringing civilisation in its wake. Few rustlers and outlaws hang around our township these days. Justice may have been harsh, in the old days, but at least it was swift. Nowadays, a man could hang around for a month, till the circuit judge came by, kicking his heels in the town jail. Sure, he can get a fair trial too, but like as not he will still end by being hanged, only he has a mite longer to ponder on his sins. Miss Esme would never have come to a town without some law and order, and I am sure glad that she did. She sings like an angel too, I hear her every Sunday at the church. The House of God is now fuller even than the saloon of a Sunday morning. Course, the saloon and the cathouse get even of a Saturday night, when it gets hotter than a jalapeno come sundown. Still and all, the men work hard and they deserve to play one night a week, to restore the body, and then get themselves to church of a Sunday to restore the soul.

Miss Esme understands that okay, so I'm not too afeared that she would think me a common man, for taking my simple pleasures. Don't worry mama, I stay away from the cathouse, Miss Esme ain't that understanding. But she don't look unkindly on a drink and a game of cards with the boys. She has learned me some reading and writing, and I'm getting on a treat. Soon I'll be able to quit the wrangling and get myself a job, like a store clerk or something down at the railway depot. Then I'll ask Miss Esme to be my bride, and build us a nice little shack on the outskirts of town. Or maybe we'll go back east, where Miss Esme's folks came from, and I'll get to work in a bank. I wouldn't want to work in the town bank here though. Even if the range outlaws and the rustlers have gone, the bank safe still gets blowed up regular as clockwork, and the merchants and ranch owners have taken to sending their money by the railroad, with armed guards. Well, Mama, I'd best be getting ready for the rodeo now. Take care now and God Bless you.

Your loving son, Jeb.

Ace-high	first class
According to Hoyle	by the book. Hoyle is a dictionary of rules for card playing games
Afeared	scared, frightened
A hog-killin' time	a really good time
All-fired	very great, immensely
Allers	always
Arbuckle's	coffee, from a popular brand
Bazoo	mouth
Beef	problem, issue
Bilk	cheat
Blow	boast
Blowhard	braggart, bully
Boot hill	cemetery
Bone yard	cemetery
Bub	brother
Bunko artist	con man
Calaboose	jail
Canned cow	canned milk
Cat house	a brothel
Cat wagon	wagon that carried prostitutes along cattle trails
Chaps	short for chaparejos; leather britches or wrap-around leggings; worn to prevent injury to the legs while chasing cattle. Popular types of chaps were woollies and shotguns
Chiseler	swindler, cheat
Cook or cookie	A cookie was the cook on the

range when cowboys drove cattle. Since all the directions a drive took were guided by the North Star, it was the camp cook's duty each night to look up, note the North Star and turn the tongue of the chuckwagon toward it. That way, the next morning, the drive would know which way to head out

Colt peacemaker
This .45-calibre has long been considered the gun that won the West. Noted for its power and reliability, it was the most popular full sized revolver of the late 1800s. Turned out by the Colt Fire Arms Manufacturing Company of Hartford, Connecticut, it sold for $17 by mail order. A classic single action revolver, it remains in production today

Cottonwood blossom
A man lynched from the limb of a tree

Cotton to
to take a liking to

Critter
creature, varmint. Sometimes used to describe a contemptible person

Crowbait
a poor-quality horse

Cussin
cursing, swearing (not generally in front of ladies) Swearwords used then were much as now, though not in general conversation

Die-up
a bad blizzard or prolonged drought that killed vast numbers of cattle, sometimes the entire herd

Deadbeat	bum, useless person
Dead man's hand	a poker hand consisting of a pair of aces and a pair of eights. Traditionally, Wild Bill Hickok was holding this hand when he was shot dead by Jack McCall. Some sources dispute the hand, saying that it really contained two jacks, not aces and two eights
Dinero	from the Spanish, a word for money.
Dry gulch	to ambush
Dude	an Easterner, or anyone in town clothes
Fish	a cowboy's rain slicker
Flannel mouth	fancy talker
Fuss	disturbance (understatement)
Get the mitten	to be rejected by a lover.
Goner	lost, dead.
Gospel sharp	a preacher
Got the bulge	have the advantage
Granger	a farmer
Hang fire	delay
Heap	a lot
Heeled	to be armed with a gun
Hoosegow	jail
Hot as a whorehouse on nickel night	very hot
Jig is up	to be found out

Kick up a rumpus	create a disturbance
Knock galley west	beat senseless
Light (or lighting) a shuck	to get out of in a hurry
Like a good'un	like someone proficient
Little Mary cowboy	the driver of the "calf wagon," a vehicle taken on some cattle drives to transport the newborn calves
Make a mash	impress
Makins	the cigarette paper and tobacco used to roll cigarettes
Mudsill	low-life
Nailed to the counter	an untruth, uncovered and proven
Oh-be-joyful	Liquor, beer, alcohol.
Plunder	personal effects
Plum tuckered	tired out
Pony Express	the brainchild of William Hepburn Russell. When the Butterfield Overland Mail Operation (St. Louis to San Francisco, a 2,800 mile route that dipped south to El Paso) was suspended in 1861, Russell convinced his partners to develop a new and simpler route from a staging area in St. Joseph, Missouri to San Francisco, using express riders to cover the ground in half the time than the

Butterfield route.

There was a $600,000 government contract at stake, so the partners took the bait and issued Russell the credit to establish his Pony Express. Then, out came the ads for young, skinny fearless riders, "Orphans preferred". Russell hired 80 such men from the hundreds of responses. The riders received a Bible, a pair of Colt revolvers and $125 a month to ride at high speed through some of the roughest and most dangerous terrain known to man. One hundred ninety stations in 5 divisions were established, 40 to 100 miles apart depending on the terrain, complete with bunk beds and feeding facilities; relay stations were established every 10 to 20 miles with small shelters, horses and stables.

On April 3, 1860, the Pony Express was formally begun - a 2,000 mile trek from St. Joseph to San Francisco. The sender had to pay $5 per half-ounce plus the regular 10-cents in U.S. postage. The Pony Express lasted 19 months and when the transcontinental telegraph reached California, the Pony Express was discontinued. But it had successfully carried 34,743 pieces of mail. Its most celebrated rider was William F. Cody.

Pony up   hurry up!

Powerful	very
Proud	glad
Quirley	roll-your-own cigarette
Revolver	Colt, Connecticut inventor and manufacturer, patented his first revolver type handgun at his plant, Patent Arms Company in Patterson, New Jersey. Using the improvements offered by Captain Samuel H. Walker of the Texas Rangers, Colt produced his 1847 model, "The Walker Colt" which proved a great success. He received a government contract for 1,100 of the revolver for use in the Mexican War and thus was able once again to open a weapons plant, this time in Hartford, Connecticut. Gun sales soared, especially during the Civil War. The next improvement was the move in 1873 from percussion cap-fired ammunition (loose powder and ball in a paper or linen cartridge) to newly invented metal cartridge containing its own primer and powder and bullet at the end of a copper or brass tube. The first pistol to fire this new ammo was called the "Peacemaker" and was often referred to as "the gun that won the West".
Ride the river	with someone to be counted on
Rip	a hell-raiser

Roostered	drunk
Rummy	a drunk
Scoop in	trick, entice
Scuttlebutt	rumours
Shank's pony	to walk or be set afoot
Shoot one's mouth off	talking too much, boasting
Skedaddle	run like hell
Soaked	drunk
Stumped	foxed, unable to comprehend
Take on	grieve, be upset by
The whole kit and caboodle	the entire thing
Tie to	rely on
Vamoose	run away

War bag   A cowboy travelled light, and stored his meagre worldly possessions in his "war bag". Inside was generally everything he owned, typically an extra set of clothes, extra ammunition, spare parts for equipment, playing cards, bill of sale for his horse, his makins and maybe a harmonica or a few precious letters.

Wells Fargo & Co.   In 1852 Henry Wells and William Fargo opened an office in San Francisco to serve the Gold rush prospectors who needed to send their Gold east. Within 15 years of founding in San Francisco Wells, Fargo and Company had absorbed or driven every serious rival out of business and had become the most important mail deliverer, bank, express agency, and stagecoach company in the West. The name of Wells Fargo is well entrenched in Western history and was so well known that miners swore only "By God and Wells Fargo."

At one time they were so efficient in the mail business that they were charging only six cents for a letter, while the Post Office was charging 25 cents, and the Post Office demanded they stop undercutting their prices. In 1850 the two partners merged their businesses with an express company owned by John Butterfield, (who later on operated a stagecoach line) and the new company was called American Express.

The importance of Stagecoaches declined after the railroad linked up to the West, but Wells Fargo acquired railroad rights as it cut back its Stagecoach operations, and it lost its lucrative mail contract in 1895 when the Federal Government took over all mail delivery services. Henry Wells made one inspection trip to San Francisco to see the new operation in 1852, William Fargo never ventured west of the Mississippi.

At the peak of their operations Wells Fargo employed a large force of Police and Detectives and more or less stopped the robbing of its Stagecoaches, by capturing about 240 what were called "Road Agents" including the famous Black Bart.

Winchester rifle

Oliver Winchester bought out the Spencer Company and then produced the famous Winchester '73 (model of 1873) rifle, arguably the most famous rifle of all time. The rifle was developed by the famous John Moses Browning of Utah, who designed many rifles, shotguns, and pistols, including the 1911 Automatic Colt Pistol (ACP) that was adopted by the U.S. Government in 1911. The original Winchester '73 was in 44-40 calibre, which meant that it was 44 calibre (actually .429 diameter) and carried 40 grains of black power. As the 45-70 was a 45 calibre slug with 70 grains of black powder, but in a much heavier rifle. The 44-40 calibre was used in six-guns as well, therefore a cowboy could use the same ammunition for both his six-gun and his rifle. In the longer barrel of the Winchester '73 the cartridge developed more power than out of the shorter barrel of the six-gun, and the much longer sight radius (the distance the front and rear sights are apart) on the rifle made "aiming" a lot easier with the Winchester rifle, over the six-gun, coupled with the fact it held more cartridges than the six-gun (which in reality was usually carried with an empty chamber under the hammer, which made it a five-shooter.)

Wind up   to settle something

CRIME

One of the most fascinating aspects of crime fiction is why, as readers, we love it so much, and why so many talented writers enjoy creating it. Perhaps it satisfies our need to make sense of the dysfunctional aspects of our society; the aberrant behaviour of individuals and groups, and allows us to empathise with the agents we authorise to police our world by proxy. Thankfully, relatively few of us actually come up against serious crime in real life, but we know that it exists and derive comfort from reading about the solving of the fictional variety, and huge satisfaction from seeing justice prevail. In writing crime, there is an opportunity to explore the universal themes of love and greed, sex and money, revenge and reconciliation, as well as the socio-pathology and psychopathology of human behaviour, from a different angle; motives for crime. It also gives all of us the chance to show how devilishly clever we are.

Crime fiction is an increasingly extensive and varied genre in contemporary writing and contains many sub genres from which the keen novelist might choose. Indeed, like science fiction and fantasy, thriller and horror, the edges that define it are frequently blurred, and there is also a broad degree of crossover. Roughly speaking, crime is understood to encompass: the whodunit or 'cosy' (featuring the gifted amateur), the private investigation or 'hardboiled' (the professional detective) and the police procedural, which is in turn sub-divided into forensic crime (fantastically popular at the time of writing) and courtroom drama. Notable heroes of 'cosies', include: Agatha Christie's Hercule Poirot and Miss Marple, Dorothy L Sayers' Lord Peter Wimsey and Chesterton's Father Brown. The 'hardboiled' P.I. is typified by Raymond Chandler's Philip Marlowe and Dashiell Hammett's Sam Spade. Lee Child's Jack Reacher and Mickey Spillane's Mike Hammer are perfect examples of more modern 'hardboiled' heroes, while Ian Rankin's Rebus and Colin Dexter's Morse are perfect examples of the police procedural hero. There are also country house mysteries and historical whodunits, like the medieval Cadfael mysteries of Ellis Peters and Lindsey Davis' Roman mysteries. This is by no means a comprehensive list, just look in the crime section of any bookstore, and there have been many heated debates about the rules and criteria governing the definition and writing of crime fiction, but it will give you an idea.

So where does the new writer start? In general terms, the whodunits, the 'cosies', will be built around a series of complex puzzles and conundrums, slowly disclosed in the plot by an large cast of characters, from every walk of life, with a few red herrings thrown in. Clues are discovered and pieced together, and the motivation and means by which the crime (often one or more murders) is committed are uncovered, leading to the solution. All is explained and revealed by the talented amateur sleuth in the denouement, at which time, the least likely suspect is often unmasked. The detective is motivated to solve the crime by an objective desire to unravel the process, using logic, deduction, and keen powers of observation. Oh and sheer nosiness. To write a successful 'cosy', the author must mirror the talents of his or her detective, and have the ability to create diverse and interesting, yet relevant characters and keep them all connected to the main plot. This can be immensely satisfying to write, if you have that sort of mind.

The 'hardboiled' PI is often an honourable outsider, who is drawn inexorably into the plot and into an intimate and alien world of professional and often underground crime and violence, and carries the reader with him. Usually written in the first person and in street vernacular, these stories bring the reader close to the thick of the action, which frequently involves physical and emotional danger for the PI, and a high degree of dramatic tension. To write a hardboiled detective, you must have a keen ear for the way that people actually speak, and be prepared to research the argot of the time and place in which your narrative is set. Your main protagonist mixes in every social circle, so your characters have to reflect that, and you will need to identify very strongly with him or her. The reader wants to care about the PI at the same time as sustaining his or her interest in the outcome of the plot.

The police procedural gives the author the chance for very technical crime writing. Here, professional policemen have dedicated technological resources and considerable manpower at their disposal, to help track down, arrest and charge a suspect or suspects, as well as to gather and present incontrovertible evidence of guilt to secure a conviction in court. These cops are subject to the frustrations of bureaucracy, the stresses of pressure from, or corruption in, high places and yet more pressure from the media and the general public. They have to consort with informers and other 'lowlifes' to gain information. Their dedication to 'nailing the perp' usually leads to a crisis in their private lives. Finding the proof also includes access to the latest advances in forensic science.

This has led to the entire sub-genre of forensic crime fiction. A special unit re-opens a cold case, or becomes involved in a live one in which the trail has gone cold, to provide hidden evidence that leads to a conviction. The expertise of one or more heroes or heroines, who may be coroners or forensic psychologists, graphologists, anthropologists, profilers and other experts will be called upon. This kind of writing takes dedicated research into, and love of, fine detail to be really convincing and then the ability to write charismatic and compelling characters to explain that detail in layman's terms.

Courtroom drama takes up the story where the others leave off and has at its heart, the tension between the accused, lawyers, judges, witnesses and ordinary members of the public serving on the jury. If you have an eye for theatre and the will to research both the law and courtroom procedure, and possibly police procedure and forensics too (you may be calling expert witnesses) this may be the sub-genre for you. Especially if you have a talent for writing convincing and engaging dialogue, since the unfolding of the plot is dependent on this. The reader has to identify with the main characters and be as convinced as the members of the jury that the right verdict has been returned, beyond reasonable doubt.

Crime fiction offers a uniquely intimate connection between writer and reader. It is a test of the intelligence and powers of reasoning of both. Readers can pit themselves against the professionals on every page, whilst never being in the slightest danger. As with all good popular fiction, the best crime writers make it look easy. Readers become attached to heroes like Morse, Rebus and Marple, Sherlock Holmes even had to be resurrected from the dead, and the writer can find him or herself in a long-term relationship with the characters he or she creates, and therefore on very good terms with the bank. So, crime fiction presents many challenges, but also huge rewards when it is done well. If you decide it is for you, use your library card to read as many of the best writers available as possible. If courtroom drama appeals to you, attend a few sessions in the public gallery of your local law courts and read the law reports in the broadsheet newspapers. Make full use of your writer's toolbox. The necessarily complex plots need careful management and you have to keep the cast of desperate characters you have imagined under close control, so let's be careful out there.

BEGINNINGS

1. I stirred the frothy cappuccino and felt guilty! I should have ordered a skinny, no fat, no sugar latte, not this luscious smooth, creamy-sweet confection, served with a liberal sprinkling of chocolate. A moment on the lips, a lifetime on the hips, were my watchwords, but my nerves were as strung out as a celeb in rehab and I began to chill at the first sip of the warm, bittersweet coffee. I really wanted this case and I could do it too! Sure, I was young and inexperienced, (not to mention gorgeous) but I had helped my dad often enough. True, his cases usually only involved scoping out the cheating partners of suspicious spouses or chasing up bad debts, but I was good at surveillance, and I could blend in better than dad with the clubbers and 'D' listers who had lately joined our clientele. At least I knew who they were from careful scrutiny of the pages of the gossip mags. Of course, I only took them to hide behind when we were undercover. Looking at me, no one would believe I took a keen interest in politics and the arts, as revealed in the 'quality' broadsheets. Actually, they'd be wrong, but that's another story.

I suddenly felt that prickly goose bump feeling when you know someone is watching you. I was the one who should be doing the watching. Omigod, had I screwed up already? Keep the paranoia to a minimum girl, save it for later, when, if my information was correct, there may be real bad guys out there, trying to get you. I took a sneaky peek at my reflection in the chrome top table, just in case it was my customary fine, frothy moustache that was exciting unwanted notice. It wasn't, but as I checked out my lip-gloss, I happened to glance up, through my exceptionally long eyelashes, expecting to meet the humorous brown eyes of the fit barista who'd served me. Surprisingly, my eyes locked onto those of a green and blue parakeet, sitting incongruously on the shoulder of the grey-haired businessman at a nearby table. I wasn't expecting that. Then the picture on the back of the newspaper, he was reading came into focus...

2. It's been twelve days, nine hours and thirty-six minutes since the most gorgeous woman I have ever seen walked into my office and crossed her silk-stockinged legs with a satin sigh. Ignoring the wooden chair, I indicated, like I didn't much care whether she sat down or not, she perched on the corner of my battered desk. "Don't try to contact me," she whispered, "I will be in touch when the time is right. I just want you to find him, and tell me where he is. Don't speak to him; don't let him know you are there; I will do the rest." I listened hard, trying to hear what it was she was really saying, but my mind kept wandering. You would expect a classy dame like this one to be bathed in some fancy French perfume. But her scent, a mixture of soap and sunshine, reminded me of nothing so much as the tow-haired kid next door. Molly and I had spent the long, hot summer of my tenth year, down by the brook, fishing for tadpoles, or in the ripening corn, looking for crickets.

But this dame was no Molly and I was more likely to be catching canaries these days; canaries ready to sing to the feds. She opened a silver cigarette case and I caught a glimpse of an engraving on the inside. She snapped it shut before I could read the inscription and tapped the end against the case before putting the cigarette to her lips, all the time never taking her eyes off mine. I leaned across to light it for her. The ice on her fingers caught the flare from the match, and spun fairy lights over the lengthening shadows on the dingy cream walls of my elite establishment. She was dazzling; I wanted to know more, to reach across and touch her silky hair, but I kept my mouth shut and my hands on the desk where I could see them. She opened her purse again and peeled off enough banknotes to keep me in java and rye for a year. I knew she was testing me. And another thing I knew for sure, this broad was trouble...

3. "No, you're right of course Chief Inspector, I wasn't actually the official holiday rep. but how could I have known that the tee shirt and shorts I grabbed from my bag that bright, sunny morning resembled the uniform that the FabTours girls wore. Yes, I could have just told him he was mistaken when he tapped me on the shoulder, and asked me if he was too late for the excursion to the traditional market and craft workshop. It was just that he looked so anxious and unhappy, and I really didn't have anything planned that day, beyond a long, cool drink by the pool and escape into *Love and Blood* by Evadne Peabody. Well, yes I suppose, I did mislead him a little, but I wouldn't

call it lying! In a split second, I had told him that he had missed the rest of the crowd, but we could catch them up. He was so grateful that I'd waited behind for him and full of praise for FabTours. Yes, well I did think he did look a bit overdressed in his shirt and tie and sports coat with the leather elbow patches. But as he blinked worriedly through those bottle bottom lenses, I thought that his feelings might be hurt if I suggested that he went up stairs to change into something more suitable for the tropical heat. His solar topee was sensible though wasn't it? Anyway, I grabbed my tote and his hand and hopped on to the bus into town. He offered me some of his sandwiches, but I do hate the smell of hard-boiled egg, don't you? The crumbs, which clung to his ginger beard, made me feel slightly nauseous, but perhaps I wouldn't have noticed that his eyebrows were definitely black otherwise. Well, he asked the driver to stop the bus for a minute, to snap the camel train. There's no need to be rude Sergeant, wouldn't you have been suspicious? No, I can't say that I'm surprised to hear you say that he is missing..."

4. I couldn't wait to pay off the cab and get inside to put my feet up. I knew that I would have to wade through the pile of junk mail and bills that would jam under the front door as soon as I pushed my key into the lock. Rover, my Persian cat (named to frighten burglars) would still be at my mother's house, getting fatter by the second, so no mews, good or otherwise, for me, but I was looking forward to a decent a cup of tea and a long, hot bath. I lugged my suitcase up the front steps (Yes, chivalry is dead, amongst cab drivers – in Ruislip anyway) and made my way into the kitchen, carelessly kicking aside the post. Now the kettle whistled and I decided to unpack while I waited for the water to heat up for my bath. If I took out the heavy things down here, I would be able to drag the bag upstairs later. First though, I had to find the little keys that rendered my luggage inviolate to international diamond smugglers and ne'r do wells. I tipped the contents of my purse out on to the carpet and scrabbled amongst the foreign coins and bits of gum, to find the tiny keys. Strangely, they seemed to be missing; just what I needed! Still, I had seen enough police shows to know that a hairpin in the right hands would soon open the locks. I wasn't known as 'Fingers' for nothing! What about luggage tampering I hear you ask. International diamond smugglers' molls are far too chic to use hairpins, so no danger there. I had no such pretensions however, and quickly found one in the muddle on the floor. Forty-five minutes later, the pesky locks yielded to my nimble fingers and the case sprung open. Oh dear! Oh dear, Oh dear, Oh dear...

5. He was bone-weary, and the sweat was sticking to the back of his shirt. It took every ounce of concentration to listen to the game of cat and mouse going on behind the two-way mirror. Ted Grander was a cool customer, no sign of sweat sullied his designer shirt and it must be ninety degrees in the interview room. He had been in there now for twelve hours and there had been at least three tag teams of good cop, bad cop going over the same ground. Joel tried to keep his instincts under tight control in a case like this. The cops were looking for a brutal serial killer, and everyone from Joe Public to the Attorney General was on their case. If this had been his case, he would have kept a lid on leaks to the press, it only made their job more difficult. Now they were looking for a quick conviction and Grander was their prime suspect.

Dr Joel Williams had been called in to profile the perp, and he had to agree that Grander was wearing that particular suit like it had been made for him. But there was something wrong here; he was way to calm and confident. So far he had displayed none of the 'tells' Joel would have expected from their perp, especially under this amount of pressure. He should be apologising for not being able to help by now. At the very least, he should be showing signs of righteous anger at his being held this long and denied access to his lawyer. He should be demanding his right to one phone call. Dr Williams didn't want to be the one to tell the boys that he didn't think that this was their guy, so he was doing this by the book, ticking the boxes. His gut feeling was that Grander was right there for a crime and he knew it, but it just wasn't this one. He knew that they could cut the case to make it fit, but he wasn't worried. Suddenly, Joel realised that this could only mean one thing, Grander knew that the killer would strike again and when, and that he would have the perfect alibi. Maybe he wasn't the brawn, just the brains. Joel spoke into Kev's earpiece...

ENDINGS

1. Sally Bolger lit a cigarette and inhaled deeply. It was hard to get her mind around the facts. She had been so convinced that Katie had been lying. Now the truth was out and Katie Peabody had been proclaimed innocent of all the charges of theft and fraud. It had been a very carefully planned and perfectly (almost) executed deception. How can I begin to repair the damage that had been done to our relationship, thought Sally, as she took another drag on her cigarette. They had known each other forever. In fact, there were times when it felt like they were sisters. Big sister always took care of little sister. Little sister always stood by and worshipped big sister. Yet she had let Katie down, just when she had most needed her trust.

DI Thompson came out of the Court building and sat on the step next to her. "I do not think you are the prerequisite 15 metres away from the door, Miss", he joked. "You do not want the passive smoke to hurt anyone." The feeble pleasantry broke the awkward silence. He put his arm around Sally's not insubstantial shoulders and said gently, "We all make mistakes." Sally looked at him and her eyes filled with tears. "How could someone have gotten hold of all her identification? They had her credit card numbers, her car number plate... that woman looked just like her on the CCTV footage?" DI Thompson stated the obvious, "It is not difficult to take someone's identity – especially when it does not appear to be of any value

– after all, poor university students do not think they have to be careful. They don't have much of a credit rating and very little money or valuables."

Katie now appeared out of the building accompanied by her attorney, the faithful Peter Davenport. She clung to his arm, looking exhausted and disoriented. Sally jumped up and ran over crying, "Katie, I am so, so very sorry". Katie looked at her with a vacant stare, "I am not Katie anymore, I do not know who I am. My identity has been stolen, it can not be given back".

2. Guy stooped and picked up the morning newspaper that had been thrown onto the ancient stone threshold. It was 8 o'clock and he was still in his robe. Guy had had a disturbed night; once again a restless spirit would not let him sleep until the early hours of the morning. He poured himself a cup of coffee, sat down and opened the paper. There on the front page was a headline feature that caught his eye.

'Police have identified and arrested the murderer of Miss Ursula Payne, aged 82. She had been brutally attacked and robbed in her home on Golf Links Road during the early hours of the morning of 15th September 2007. Items of value known to have been taken include jewellery, several valuable pictures and first edition books.

This is one of a series of recent burglaries targeting the affluent elderly in the Bournemouth area. The police have given this investigation the highest priority, as the incidents have been increasingly frequent and violent.

The alleged attacker has been identified as Simon Yates, a 35 year-old handyman, currently of no fixed abode. Mr Yates was found to have one of Ursula's diamond earrings and several valuable books in his possession, and is known to have taken art appreciation courses at the local university.

This reporter has discovered that a key witness in this investigation is the well-known psychic Guy Smyth. Detective Superintendent Vincent Ray has reluctantly confirmed this fact. It is believed that the psychic was able to lead the police to a lock up garage, where important forensic evidence was found, including the lead pipe that was used to batter Miss Payne'.

Guy put the paper down and smiled to himself. It amused him to think how simple it all had been and would still be. All those silly old dears - how they loved their readings, and all he had to do was tell them a few true facts and lots of fluffy rubbish. His psychic luncheons were usually a very good day out with nice food and drink, added to which his psychic services provided him with some declarable income. And oh how the old ladies did like to show him all their pretty bibelots.

"Time for a new MO", Guy muttered to himself, "And I do wish Ursula would stop twittering on – I need my sleep."

3. The garden, usually so cheerful and full of life, today looked incredibly sad. It was as beautifully tended as always, but the spirit of the place was an unhappy one. No insects were buzzing, even the robin that owned the garden had left to visit relatives.

Megan sat on the bench near the roses, flipped open her mobile and rang Jason at his office. After the usual exchange of greetings, he asked "Any news on your Hen & Chicks?" Megan was sure that he was trying to irritate her on purpose. Jason knew that she always afforded her creation the dignity of its Latin name; *Papaver somniferum phillipsii*. Actually, it was a good tactic on his part, it was a relief to feel annoyed rather than desperate and helpless. "Yes that rather tedious detective, Miller, seems to have a bit of lead. He did not give any details but sent me an ambiguous text message – something to do with Kew. When I rang him at the station I got the usual run around from the other detective, Whatsit Woods. Why will no one take this seriously?" whined Megan.

"Patience Prudence", cautioned Jason "No use getting the police's backs up." "But it is so important', started Megan winding up again, "with Chelsea coming up and I am the very first to get this shape of pods. Oh if only we had registered it on the DNA database." "I know, I know, I have heard it all before", interrupted Jason, "I will go and find Miller myself, you just sit tight – or better yet go and pull a weed. Whatever you do, do not speak with the police, reporters or anyone else you have not known for at least 15 years." Going into the Kew Garden offices Jason found Miller in conference with a middle-aged woman in a white lab coat. His back looked as dapper and designer as his front, so out of place in the world of nature. When Miller saw Jason approaching he spoke a few words to his companion. Then, turning, beckoned to Jason to join him in a quiet corner, where they sat together on a small sofa. Jason felt uncomfortable having his personal space violated.

"What news?" asked Jason squeezing himself into the end of the sofa. "I have solved the mystery", said Miller quietly "Quite simple really, and it has nothing to do with a competitor stealing this new variety to show." Miller went on to explain that he had asked Kew to analyze the remaining seed pod. They had confirmed, what he had suspected; that Megan's creation had not only thrown up a unique pod formation; but was also the source of very superior opium. The latex was found to contain 25% morphine, 10% higher than other varieties. The police suspected that the first theft had been a bit of joke by young Ernst Andrews. Then he and his school mates had extracted the juice to see if it would give them a high. It was then that the value of the poppy was discovered – it was worth millions to the drug barons. Jason rang Megan and told her. "The good news is that you do not have to worry that your little hen will be marketed by another grower. The bad news is we will not be able to cultivate it either – unless under licence for a pharmaceutical company."

4. This wood could do with a bit of elbow grease and some good beeswax polish, thought Mrs C as she took her place at the bottom of the table next to the Vicar. Who'd have thought it, Lady Mary dead, and the whole family, if you could call it that, gathered for the reading of the will? She would hardly have recognised Mr Simon, or Mr George and Miss Lizzy looked no better than she should be. As for that sister of hers, chalk and cheese, she supposed. Vultures! Not that there can be much to leave, she mused to herself, looking up at the faded squares and oblongs where once, valuable paintings had hung against the threadbare but handsome, silk wallpaper. Shabby now, she sniffed disapprovingly. Still, it was nice to think that Lady M had appreciated all her years of service at the Hall. As she had told her neighbour, "You could have knocked me down with a feather when the letter arrived from Lady M's lawyer."

That gentleman now cleared his throat and stood at the head of the table. Before he could open his mouth however, there was some kind of a disturbance outside the door, and that nosy reporter girl stood at the threshold, accompanied by two policemen. "I'm sorry Mr Harcourt" she said, coming right in, and standing beside him, "The reading of the will have to be postponed." "Now look here!" shouted Mr George, getting to his feet. But the young woman raised her hand to silence him.

"As I suspected, Lady Mary Danvers did not die of natural causes, but was murdered in this very house, and the murderer is here in this room. Before I explain how I know this and the guilty man or woman is exposed, let me take you back to the night three weeks ago, when you all arrived to celebrate Lady Mary's birthday. It was then that she discovered that Evangeline had not, as was supposed, spent the last ten years as a Sister of Mercy at the Convent in Colchester, but had in fact been serving at Her Majesty's pleasure for soliciting and bigamy. When faced with her guilty secret, Evangeline broke down and confessed that it was not she, but her twin sister, Miss Elizabeth Danvers who had committed the crime, and that she had agreed to go to prison in her stead, under threat of violence from their older brother, George. Mr Simon Danvers claims to have been abroad, seeking his fortune in South Africa, but Lady Mary knew that he has been no further than Southend, where he has been running an illegal gambling den, and topping up his tan at the ManTanFantastic salon in Bridge Street. Mr George Danvers has been blackmailing all three with threat of exposure and the ruin of the family's good name. All of you feared that Lady Mary would disinherit you when, on that fateful night and in some distress she summoned her solicitor Mr Harcourt to the Hall. You each in turn tried to curry favour with her, by revealing the dark secrets of the other two. You each had access to the poison, which was kept in the housekeeper's cupboard for the disposal of the infestation of rats in the attics. Each of you I know might expect to be exposed as the killer, but I can tell you that Lady Mary did not die of the considerable amount of poison that was found at post mortem and in the quadruple brandy beside her bed. She had been suffocated, and you Mr Harcourt suffocated her." "Well I never" sniffed Mrs C.

5. Epilogue: The corpse was finally buried on the 22nd of November. The church organ played and everyone stood as the coffin was brought in and placed in front of the altar. The huge flower arrangements overpowered rather than enhanced the small stone chapel. It was much better suited to simple bouquets of daisies, lilacs and red campion, filled out with foliage hacked from some kind soul's garden. But the funeral must be as beautiful as the corpse. Polly was buried in the ancient crypt as she had always imagined, fully embalmed so that her exquisite looks would be preserved as long as possible. The less charitable amongst the congregation thought that all the cosmetic procedures she had in life probably assisted this. Simon was heard to remark, "Polly was a patchwork of silicone, stitch scars, fillers and botox so there really is nothing to decay". The atmosphere was more reality show than reality.

Keith Beechwood returned to Honiton and continued his life coaching practice. His reputation for counselling the 50+s to retool and start new careers was only enhanced by this incident. Soon afterwards Keith wrote a book on the experience of reinventing Harry and it was on the best seller list for 10 months.

After the funeral the Chief Medical Examiner found his office a lonely place. He frequently spoke of Polly to his students, always insisting that he was the last and truest of her admirers. When asked to explain why, he told the story of how her body reflected her life and her nature. He had found beauty in her imperfections the signs of motherhood, stress and impending middle age so carefully covered up in life. Polly never understood that a true lover needed the reassurance of such weaknesses, to be the one who gave unconditional support when life's tragedies inevitably struck.

Harry stayed in the City for the next ten years. He bought a two-bedroom flat in Docklands, a Mercedes Benz and a beautiful trophy wife. He became known as the guy that could do a Dr Who morph, as often as needed. In the end Harry was even awarded an MBE for his services to the Prime Minister's favourite charity.

CLASSIC WHODUNIT

Actress
Adventuress
Arsenic
Aspidistra

Backstairs
Boat train
Brandy
Busybody
Butler

Church porch
Clues
Companion
Cook
Country house
Curate
Cyanide

Dagger
Decanter
Dinner
Disguise

Family Solicitor
Fast getaway car
Flower arrangement
Foreigner
Friend of the family
Gamekeeper
Garden
Gardener
Gun

Hat
Hotel
Housekeeper

Imposter
Intruder
Investments

Letter
Limp
Loot

Maid of all work
Mail train
Milk train
Mirror
Motor car
Moustache
Murder

Newspaper
Notebook

Orchard

Pearls
Poison
Police Officer
Police Station
Poor relation
Porter
Post
Postman

Railway Station
Railway timetable

Scotland Yard
Service Revolver
Shopkeeper
Shot
South of France
Strangulation

Tea
Telephone
Title
Tradesmen

Uncle

Valet
Vicar

Waitress
Will

CLASSIC HARDBOILED

Babe	woman
Bean-shooter	gun
Behind the eight-ball	in a tight spot
Berries	dollars
Big house	jail
Big one, the	death
Blow	leave
Blower	telephone
Boob	dumb guy
Boozehound	drunk
Bop	kill
Bracelets	handcuffs
Breeze	leave, breeze off, get lost
Broad	woman
Bucket	car
Bump gums	to talk about nothing
Bump off	kill
Burn powder	fire a gun
Button	face, nose, end of jaw
C	$100, a pair of Cs = $200
Cabbage	money
Caboose	jail
Can	jail, car
Canary	woman singer
Century	$100
Cheaters	sunglasses
Chick	woman
Chin music	punch on the jaw

Chippy	woman of easy virtue
Chisel	to swindle or cheat
Clammed	close-mouthed (clammed up)
Clean sneak	escape without leaving clues
Clip joint	night-club where the prices are high and the patrons are fleeced
Conk	head
Cop	detective, even a private one
Corn	Bourbon
Crate	car
Dame	woman
Dance	to be hanged
Dib	share (of the proceeds)
Dick	detective (usually private)
Dip the bill	have a drink
Dish	pretty woman
Dive	a cheap place
Dizzy with a dame, to be	to be in love with a woman
Do the dance	to be hanged
Doll, dolly	woman
Dope	drugs, of any sort
Dough	money
Drift	go, leave
Drill	shoot
Duck soup	easy, a piece of cake
Fade	go away, get lost
Fin	$5 bill

Finger	identify
Flat	broke
Flippers	hands
Fry	to be electrocuted
From nothing	"I know from nothing"
Gams	legs
Give the third	interrogate (third degree)
Grab (a little) air	put your hands up
Grand	$1000
Half, A	50 cents
Hash house	cheap restaurant
Have the bees	to be rich
Horn	telephone
House peeper	house/hotel detective
Ice	diamonds
Jane	woman
Java	coffee
Jaw	talk
Joe	coffee
Kisser	mouth
Kitten	woman
Large	$1,000
Lettuce	folding money
Lid	hat
Lip	criminal lawyer

Marbles	pearls
Moll	girlfriend
Mouthpiece	lawyer
Newshawk	reporter
Pan	face
Peach	inform
Peeper	detective
Pigeon	stool-pigeon
Pins	legs (especially a woman's)
Plug	shoot
Pump metal	shoot bullets
Puss	face
Ringers	fakes
Rod	gun
Sap	dumb guy, blackjack
Sawbuck	$10 bill (a double sawbuck is a $20 bill)
Schnozzle	nose
Scratch	money
Shamus	(private) detective
Shiv	knife
Sing	confess
Sister	woman
Skipout	leave a hotel without paying
Skirt	woman
Sleuth	detective
Slug	(n) bullet (v) to knock unconscious

Smoked	drunk
Snatch	kidnap
Snooper	detective
Snort	a short drink (spirits)
Snow-bird	(cocaine) addict
Sock	punch
Soup	Nitroglycerine
Spill	talk, inform
Spinach	money
Spitting	talking
Spondulix	money
Square	honest; on the square: telling the truth
Stiff	corpse
Tail	shadow, follow
Take the air	leave
Ticket	P.I. license
Tin	badge
Tomato	pretty woman
Trap	mouth
Two bits	$25, or 25 cents.
Up-and-down	a look
Wire	news
Wise, to be	to be in the know
Yap	mouth
Yard	$100

POLICE PROCEDURAL

ABH (UK)		actual bodily harm
ADW (US)		assault with a deadly weapon
APB (US)		all points bulletin
ARV (UK)		armed response vehicle
Assume the position		spreadeagle against wall to be searched
At large (US)		unaccounted for
Back up (US/UK)		to assist another officer
Badge (US)		identification
Bail (US/UK)		money or security bond posted with the Court to guarantee an appearance
Beat (UK)		Geographical area of patrol assignment
Blag (UK)		violent robbery
BOLO (US)		Be On the Lookout for
Book (US)		to formally gather information after an arrest
Brief (UK)		solicitor or barrister
CID (UK)		criminal investigation department
CJ (US)		county jail
Codes (US)	**Code-1:**	No particular hurry; whenever convenient
	Code-2:	Some urgency- get moving
	Code-3:	All out emergency; lights and sirens

Code-4:	Under control, no further assistance necessary
Code-5:	Stakeout
Code-6:	On foot; walking patrol
Code-7:	Meal Breaks
Code-33:	Emergency situation-emergency radio traffic only
CPS (UK)	Crown Prosecution Service
Custody sergeant (UK)	officer in charge of cells
DA (US)	district attorney (prosecution)
Defense lawyer (US)	lawyer on behalf of accused
DOA (US/UK)	dead on arrival
DOB	date of birth
Drugs Squad (UK)	department investigating drugs crime
Duty solicitor (UK)	lawyer on behalf of accused (defence)
Felon (US)	someone arrested for, or convicted of a felony crime
Felony (US)	serious crime, with a potential prison sentence
GOA (US)	gone on arrival
Homicide (US)	division responsible for investigating murder

Identity parade (UK)	line-up for witness to identify suspect
Infraction (US)	violation of law
Lawyer up (US)	ask for, or be represented by an attorney
Light `em up (US)	activate emergency lights and siren
Line-up (US)	daily pre-work meeting of the patrol team
Loaded (US)	under the influence of a narcotic
Local Nick (UK)	local police station
Manslaughter (US)	unlawful killing, with mitigating circumstances
Miranda (US)	the suspect's rights, as read on arrest
Misd (US)	misdemeanour
MO (UK/US)	modus operandii
Murder One (US)	deliberate murder
Narcotics (US)	drugs squad
Pat down (US)	do a cursory search for weapons at a detention or arrest
Patrol car (UK US)	
Perp (US)	perpetrator
Photo lineup (US)	group of 6 photos, with one of the suspect, for witnesses to identify

PO (US)	probation
Police custody in (UK)	under arrest
Prime suspect (UK)	most likely perpetrator of crime
QE (UK)	Queen's evidence. To testify on behalf of the state
QOA (US)	quiet on arrival
Sorted (UK)	organized, finished
SOCO (UK)	scene of crime officer (forensic)
State's evidence (US)	to testify on behalf of the state
Station (US)	police station
UTL (US)	unable to locate
Vice (UK/US)	department investigating vice
Witness Protection Scheme (US)	in which prosecution witnesses are hidden for their own protection

Forensic

Animation

computer graphic and audio visual recreations of crime and accident scenes

Arsenic

poison

Asphyxiation

suffocation

Ballistics

the study of guns and bullets

Blood splatter patterns

murder scene evidence

Bridge

denture anchored to teeth on either side of missing teeth

Cap

crownwork, dental appliance

Carbon monoxide

colourless, odourless, very toxic gas made up of carbon and oxygen

Cartridge case

cylindrical case of pasteboard, metal or the like, for holding a complete charge of powder, and often, also the bullet for a rifle, machine gun or small arm

Chromatography

method for separating mixtures based on differences in the speed at which they migrate over or through a stationary phase

Composite	image of a face made up from separate facial parts
Coroner	public official who investigates by inquest any death not due to natural causes
Crown	enamel cover (on teeth)
Cyanide	chemical compound comprised of carbon and nitrogen
DNA	genetic material used for identification
Electrocution	death brought about by electricity
Electrophesis	method of separating large molecules (such as DNA fragments or proteins) from a mixture of similar molecules
Femur	thighbone
Fibre	fine, threadlike piece matter made from such threads.
Filling	dental appliance consisting of any of various substances (as metal or plastic) inserted into a prepared cavity in a tooth

Fluorescent   bright vivid colour that glows under a black light.

Formaldehyde   pungent gas; in liquid form, used as an antiseptic, disinfectant and fixative for tissues

Haemorrhage   bleed severely

Hologram   laser-created photograph that creates a three-dimensional image

Hyoid   Indent notch or dent left on paper due to the force from the tip of a pen when writing

Hypostasis   pooling of blood as it accumulates at the lowest parts of the body- a method of determining the position of the body at/after death

Hypothermia   when the core body temperature falls below normal

Laceration   a rough cut

Luminal   spray used to enhance fingerprints

Odontology   the science of teeth

PCR

(polymerase chain reaction) method for amplifying a DNA base sequence and can be used to detect the existence of the defined sequence in a DNA sample

Polygraph

lie detector i.e. instrument that records several physiological processes simultaneously (e.g. pulse rate and blood pressure and respiration and perspiration)

Rigor mortis

stiffening of the body muscles after death

Strangulation

respiration stopped by compression of the air passage.

Thin-layer

chromatography procedure used to identify drugs of abuse in urine

Tissue

aggregate of cells having a similar structure and function.

Trauma

physical injury or wound caused by an external force of violence, which may cause death

Courtroom

Accused one who is charged with a crime

Acquit to find a defendant not guilty in a criminal trial

Admissible evidence allowed in court

Arraign calling upon accused by name, reading to him the charges in the arrest documents, demanding of him whether he pleads guilty or not guilty entering his plea

Arrest to deprive of liberty by legal authority

Contempt of court any act calculated to embarrass, hinder, or obstruct the court in administration of justice or which is calculated to lessen its authority or its dignity

Continuance postponement until a later date

Defence the lawyers acting for the defendant, presenting evidence of his innocence

Defendant the accused

Direct Examination   the initial questioning of a
                           witness by the party who
                           called him or her

Dock   place where the accused stands
                           or sits during the trial

Expert witness   one who has special
                           expertise to present evidence
                           pertinent to the case

Evidence   all the means by which a
                           matter of fact, the truth of
                           which is submitted for
                           investigation, is established
                           or disproved.

Habeas corpus   a writ commanding the
                           person holding a prisoner
                           in custody to bring the
                           prisoner before the court
                           to determine whether the
                           prisoner is legally detained

Jury   12 people selected from the
                           community to hear
                           evidence and decide a
                           criminal case

Juvenile   a person under the age of 18.

Objection   a protest or exception
                           made against an action by
                           the other side.

Perjury a criminal offence; giving a false statement under oath.

Plea statement made by the defendant either as to his guilt or innocence

Prosecution the lawyers acting on behalf of the state in a trial to present the case for conviction

Reasonable Doubt the degree of certainty beyond which the state must prove its accusations to obtain a criminal conviction

Sentence the judgment formally pronounced by the judge setting the punishment for the crime

Subpoena a process commanding a witness to appear before a court.

Transcript a written, verbatim record of a legal proceeding

Verdict the formal decision or finding of guilt or innocence made by a judge

Witness one who testifies to what he has seen, heard or otherwise observed

133

Horror

From the earliest days of the novel, stories designed to shock, frighten, and even terrify the pants off the reader have been amongst the most avidly read in popular fiction. Horror is a broad-ranging genre with the inevitable overlaps with science fiction and fantasy, thriller and suspense; even romance. From 19th century Gothic horror writers, such as Edgar Allen Poe; *The Fall of the House of Usher, The Pit and the Pendulum, The Masque of the Red Death*; Mary Shelley; *Frankenstein* and Bram Stoker; *Dracula*, to Dean Kootz, Clive Barker and Stephen King in modern times, authors have found horror to be a vehicle for examining philosophical and metaphysical concepts, as well as aspects of myth, legend and the dark archetypes of the supernatural. By no means all horror writing depicts extreme and explicit violence; it is a superb medium for psychological terror as well as blood and gore. Horror fiction can be a specialist area for a writer of imagination, or an exploratory device for novelists to work outside their usual confines to consider the less comfortable aspects of the human psyche. For example, many would consider Henry James' *The Turn of the Screw*, a spine-chilling but bloodless thriller, to be in this category, but would hardly define James as a horror writer.

Man has no natural predators that we know of, but that doesn't mean we aren't at risk. Some of the earliest fables, tales told around the campfire, while shrieks outside its light reminded the traveller that he must stay awake, or risk dying at the claws of some unseen creature of the night, form the basis of many modern examples of the genre. As a writer you have a pretty free hand when it comes to narrative, plot and character. Many authors have tried to find a way to express the greatest of human dreads – pure evil. Still others have taken the subject to look closely at the consequences of a world without taboo, an amoral world where creatures exist without any comprehension of right and wrong. Scientific advance, (which, as laymen we don't understand) and the scientists driven mad in intellectual pursuit of the impossible, as well as creatures older than time itself; all have been grist to the horror mill. Ghosts, ghouls, vampires, witchcraft and sorcery all feature heavily, as well as the monsters that lurk in the subconscious and the all-powerful dinosaurs that roamed the earth before man became the dominant species. Could they still be living somewhere, biding their time until they return and take back their inheritance?

For a new writer, horror does present some interesting possibilities. We are often advised to write about what we know. Nothing could be simpler; we all have a powerful knowledge of the monsters of myth and fairytale from our earliest childhood. Witches, goblins, fairies and the bogeymen with whom non-pc parents frightened children into good behaviour, are all taken from the same Pandora's box of myth and legend as vampires and werewolves, demons and trolls. So there is no shortage of archetypes from which to draw. But perhaps the most frightening monster of all is man himself and that of which he is capable. Academics and psychologists have suggested that the monsters with which we scare ourselves are metaphors for real threats and dangers to which we are subject.

Vampires can then be seen as sexual predators against which young women must be warned. (Vampires are grimly seductive to adolescent girls; dark, handsome and apparently irresistible) Witches may represent the threat that the wisdom and strength of women presents to men, especially young women, with great sexual power and the mystery of motherhood at their command, and old women who are neither desirable nor subject to their emotional control. Perhaps this accounts for the popularity of erotic horror as a sub-genre? It would seem that only middle-aged matrons do not frighten them! In any event, these ideas offer splendid opportunities for the modern fiction writer.

The aim is to stimulate the adrenalin of the reader, the flight or fight mechanism, with the power of your imagination. Phobias can be a useful inspiration too. In essence, horror is simultaneously repellent and attractive and you must draw on vocabulary and dramatic tension to push the boundaries of the acceptable and recreate that effect in your work. Early horror fiction was often set against backdrops that were, in themselves frightening; dark and brooding castles, deep caverns and impenetrable forests. Modern horror tends to take advantage of the added frisson that comes with finding a monster in the most ordinary of circumstances – the vampire in the shopping mall, or the ghost in cyberspace. The use of everyday vocabulary, peaceful locations, and unsuspecting victims all help to build tension and the 'Look out behind you' factor that is essential to effective scare-mongering.

This genre does have the advantage that it is largely work of the imagination, but if your story is set in a specific period or location, or involves technology; you will still need to do accurate research. Your frightener will be more credible if the reader knows the rest of your story to be true, or can at least check the facts. Stephen King, Peter Straub, Anne Rice and Dean Kootz are among many contemporary masters of this dramatic device and their work should form part of the extensive background reading you will want to do. Look for your inspiration in the unexplained and the surprising, urban legend is the stuff of modern horror, but please, whatever you do, don't go alone at dead of night, to explore the locked room in the old empty house on the edge of town…

Beginnings

1. The handle felt cool in his hands, and he held the blade up to the light. The edge was so sharp it was almost invisible. The knife was his chosen weapon – silent and deadly, and involved. You could not pretend to yourself that you were disconnected from the act when you plunged it deep into another's flesh.

He had used this knife for every one of his seven murders. He was not afraid to call it murder. He did not deceive himself. He had taken the lives of seven men; in cold blood, some would say. How strange then, that he could feel the blood hot and strong, pulsing through his body at the very memory of his work. He did not call it revenge, or execution, even to himself, though he was certain that at the heart of the matter there was justice. He felt no regret, no remorse. He knew that the police would look for the murder weapon, but he would not discard it. If they found him they would find him with his knife in his hand and the victory would be theirs. But they would not find him. There was nothing to connect him to his victims, absolutely nothing, except that he cared nothing for any of them. He had chosen them at random, only as representatives of their kind, not as individuals and they had nothing in common with one another. He tested the blade against his own flesh and resumed stropping it against the strap held between his wrist and elbow. He found the action soothing, like being rocked in his mother's arms. He could almost remember that creature who had given him life. She had raised him well and shown him his limitations, as well as his strengths, and it was this knowledge that would be his protection against discovery. He knew himself, heart and blood and sinew, mind and body. No, he was not invincible, but he was invisible...

2. She woke with a crick in her neck. Drool had glued her cheek to the page of dense type in the tome before her on the desk. It was past midnight and she had fallen asleep hours ago. Panic blurred her vision and shot adrenalin through her veins as she thought about the test in the morning. Her heart was beating far too fast. She had wasted so much time, and now the dawn was only a matter of hours away. She moved to the basin and splashed her face with cold water. Maybe, she thought whimsically, the words had been drawn into her brain by osmosis as she slept. She made herself some strong coffee, and sat down at the desk ready to start again. The light flickered as she adjusted the angle of the lamp. Damn, she would have to go down to the cellar and fetch a new bulb, now, before this

one blew. If she didn't catch it in time, the trip switch would be activated and she would lose all the power. The old house creaked around her, settling for the night and somewhere, she could hear a shutter rattling, trying to open to the icy wind from the sea that cut through the trees to enter every crack in the clapperboard house on the bluff. Damn again, she didn't have time for this. She felt tired and cranky, and not for the first time she asked herself why she felt compelled to set herself impossible goals. If she hadn't been so driven, David might not have packed, loaded up the SUV and driven out of her life. He had called her obsessive and perhaps she was. She was appalled to find herself tempted to close the books and take a walk outside in the moonlight; watch the Atlantic waves crashing against the rocks below. She shook herself, if she didn't ace this test tomorrow she would lose the improbable, wonderful house that her grandfather had built with his bare hands and with it her past and her future…

3. Karolyn awoke gasping for breath in the silence of the night. The room seemed oppressively close after the gentle night breeze coming off the grey-green sea of her dream. Her skin felt clammy, with sweat, where moments before it had been bathed in the light sea-spray carried on the wind. The greenish illumination of the figures on her alarm clock blinked the hour, 2.31. It seemed to her, as she had stood at the water's edge, that time was irrelevant in the gentle, grey moonlight. She had felt such a sense of complete peace and harmony. Now the anxiety of the inevitable insomnia that would follow her abrupt awakening began to tease her. What had pulled her from her deep sleep? She lay listening

in the darkness for any sound that could have penetrated her sub-conscious. Could she hear the hum of the refrigerator downstairs, and the sound of water in the pipes? Was a window banging somewhere or perhaps a trapped bird fluttered in the great chimney, trying to find a way out. Had the book she had been reading fallen from the night table with a soft thwack? Her heart began to beat a little faster, but she could hear nothing but the pulse thrumming gently in her ears. Perhaps, in this remote country place the cry of a night animal, long since gone on its way, had disturbed her. Maybe someone had tried to break in. Her heart began to race as she reached for the light switch and swung her legs out of bed. Was that a creak on the stair? As her bare feet reached the soft carpet and searched automatically for her slippers, she glanced downward and her now frantically beating heart missed a beat. It couldn't be, there on the carpet, a damp footprint and soft sand between her toes....

4. Marcus had studied the firm's meteoric rise on the stock market for months now; he was surprised how little press interest it had generated. Indeed, despite his having the inside track, it was unbelievably difficult to find out anything very much at all about Ceres Inc. He had failed to discover what, if anything, besides billions of dollars, they actually made in the great opaque glass structure in the middle of the city desert. That was what made it all the more extraordinary, so extraordinary that he could still scarcely believe it, that he was even now on his way to meet the fabled girl-genius behind this legendary company. He had seen photographs of her of course, on the Internet, although she still hadn't made the cover of Forbes. There was no doubt she was outstandingly beautiful, and so young to have achieved so much. Marcus smiled wryly; he could not deny that he had always been a sucker for that particular mix of classic elegance, fawn-like fragility and long, long legs. He couldn't decide whether he was most looking forward to meeting her, or to discussing the dream job for which he was being interviewed. Who was he kidding?

How James had fixed it he would never know, but he owed him big-time. When his old roommate had called to say that she would be happy to meet him today, he been beyond elated. Now as he travelled to the award-winning building in which rumour had it, the Ceres' stunning state-of-the-art offices were housed, the emotional cocktail of adrenalin and pleasure anticipated left him shaken. He barely heard the cold whisper at first, above the noise of the train, and then he assumed that it was addressed to someone else, but when it was repeated, this time using his half-remembered childhood nickname, his entire attention was engaged...

5. The rich smell of the soft loam and the shush of the burrowing insects filled her senses with the power and strength of life. The earth was alive with night creatures feasting on the decaying flesh of the bodies all around her. She sighed softly; ah the circle of life, birth, death decay, life, she thought to herself. She had read of these things in the volumes of natural science in her grandfather's fabled library. The books were all gone now, taken by Philistines and burned on pyres, or shut away in great steel vaults with no locks, away from prying eyes. But the knowledge remained, that could not be destroyed as long as she lived -

and that would be forever. Alas, she would never experience the circle of life. Her body would never nourish the maggots and the beetles. Her smooth young flesh would never be torn apart by rats and foxes, or her eyes pecked by the circling crows. She would never lie in her grave, empty of all that she had been, a mound of white bones, and a grinning skull. Her lustrous black hair would never be woven, with moss and feathers into intricate nests for families of field mice.

'Thank Hades,' she said aloud. Her long white, hands with their red-tipped nails brushed the earth aside as the casket swung open. She brushed the dust from her clothes and walked quickly through the moonlit darkness towards the cemetery gates. A way down the highway the neon sign flickered and she smiled. The motel might not be the last word in luxury, but it was a place to wash up (she scrubbed up pretty well though she said so herself) and to change her clothes and keep a few small mementoes, a place to take her date later perhaps? What more did a girl need?

Cassia moved quickly down the side of the highway, keeping to the shadows. Soon she began to feel hungry, and the scent of warm blood pulsing through healthy young bodies replaced the smell of the cold earth in her nostrils. She ran her tongue over her full lips and just touched the tips of the small, sharp, white teeth...

Endings

1. Fredrick turned to Billy – her black hair was filthy and in knots, her expression frozen with terror. He put his arm

around her and she fell into his shoulder gasping out dry sobs of despair. Quietly he said, "It's over for now, let me take you home." Billy looked up and nodded. She noticed his arm covered in acid burns and lacerations, their makeshift weapon had worked, but had left its mark.

They climbed slowly and painfully into the red convertible. Driving back to their little yellow house, the landscape looked exactly like it had two weeks before. The Spanish moss still fell from the trees. The row of look-alike suburban houses was still bathed in the Florida sunshine, the lawns being watered through automatic sprinklers. Beautifully coiffed and manicured desperate housewives drove by in people-carriers. Youngsters rode around the streets on bikes, and whizzed around on skateboards. Everywhere, the atmosphere was one of domestic normalcy, the confident expectation of a future – generation after generation.

But now Fredrick knew the truth, a terrible, unchangeable truth and nothing would be the same again. It would be his and Billy's secret and they would take it to their graves. Both knew that this would only be a matter of months, or at best a year away. The gas that they had inhaled in the cave would slowly destroy their lungs; no doubt this would be put down to asbestos poisoning. Together they would keep the truth from the world, as one protects a child from the knowledge of their impending death from leukaemia. What is the point in killing hope when nothing can be done to avoid the inevitable destruction? Dromos was back in his lair but that was not the end of it… nothing would ever end this.

2. I look up at Damon with longing. He would kill me and this would sustain him for a while at least. My clothes are torn and dishevelled. I am mutilated and violated. My hands are covered with welts and scratches and cuts. Small burn marks dot my arms where his cigarette has scorched my skin. Even my fingernails are torn from their beds.

Whilst torturing me Damon pontificated about the reality and truth of evil. "Evil," he said, tightening my bonds around my chest, "is not just the absence of good, it is whole and substantial in itself." I gasped for breath, hoping he would not notice how I had enlarged my rib cage. "The media is so misleading," Damon continued, "All this foolishness about friendly vampires and ghouls. We do not harbour a sense of remorse or guilt. It leads foolish souls like you to become our prey, always thinking that we can be reformed. Your subjugation and destruction are as necessary to me, as your need for love is to you. The gratification is both spiritual and physical." I replied quietly, "You cannot mean that, what about the need to procreate to protect the female and child, is this not the most primal of instincts?"

Damon smiled with cynicism and hidden wisdom "Perhaps once, but even humanity has evolved beyond that – now the need to compete and win is equally driving." Damon bent down over me and kissed my hand. "I will remember you," he whispered.

I ran from the darkness of the crypt-like cellar. Relief flooded over me, I had not believed I would survive the horrors of the night. My desperate struggle with the beautiful, sadistic Damon was over. I will never know how I managed to loose the bounds and to escape. At first I thought, good does triumph over evil, he subconsciously cared enough to let me go. Then I remembered Damon was also safe to live another day, gorged on my blood and humiliation.

3. Epilogue: In July 2008, Wonderland Venture Capital decided not to invest in the 'Diet Easy' Plan. Having done an extensive due diligence on Forever Thin Laboratories, it was decided their procedures were not rigorous enough to pass FDA regulations. Also the initial test results on humans did indeed show dramatic 'no effort' weight loss. But the magic fat-eating worms seemed to have mysterious undisclosed side effects.

Simon Castel, the principal scientist of Forever Thin Laboratories never successfully patented the 'Diet Easy' Plan. He was not able to, or would not sufficiently describe the process and unique ingredients to justify the award of a patent. In 2009 he closed down the laboratories and went to work for L'Oreal.

Annabel Rhys-Jones never regained the 30 kg of weight she had lost. In fact she continued to lose weight regardless of how much she ate. She soon tired of hearing "Annabelle you look marvellous!" Her size 0 body did not improve her quality of life, rather the opposite. She mourned the loss of her curves and cursed her love/hate relationship with food. Annabelle's nightmare of seething masses of maggots crawling over her body became more and more recurrent, until she was convinced that she saw them even in the light of day; tiny, transparent beings on her skin, invisible to others, eating her alive. Annabel died a few months after the experiment ended, having overdosed herself with a well-known sheep drench used for getting rid of worms.

Rimini Laughton, the unscrupulous and devious deputy to Simon, stole the colony of magic fat-eating worms and their nutrient formula. She re-invented the product(s) under the new name of 'diet caterpillars' with the slogan 'The secret of being an eternally beautiful Butterfly'. Rimini took the process a step further, discovering a way to control the worm population and thus the weight loss. However the control drench, could not, or was deliberately designed not to, entirely eradicate the 'caterpillars'. Once infested all clients were hooked into the system, quite literally for life. By the time the FDA discovered how it worked, millions of people's health was at risk. Rimini disappeared with $5 billion and somebody else's husband.

4. On that cold January afternoon Maria came through the surgery door, all smiles with her beige teeth showing below a faint moustache. Dr Adam looked up from the report; he could not remember why he had ever thought her attractive. His first impression had been of a rounded, vulnerable woman whose Madonna beauty was faded but still alluring.

Now the mask was stripped away, Maria appeared a grotesque figure, like a celebrity with too much cosmetic surgery. Her body had been transformed from menopausal to that of a fertility goddess. It was all breasts and hips moving youthfully with a swinging gait, responding to the hormones that were making her pelvis supple in preparation for the birth. But above and around her torso, were all the signs of middle-aged melt down; the lined face and saggy jowls. Her hands were covered in liver spots and veins, her arms floppy and her feet covered in bunions and corns.

"How are you today Maria?" he asked, knowing full well that they both knew how she was. "You tell me Doctor," replied Maria, in her low soft voice "But I am sure that I am pregnant, I can feel my womb coming alive." She sensed his hesitancy and this made her suddenly straighten up and become alert. "What is wrong Dr Adams, are you not pleased with your success? Your unsurpassed skill has given me a the gift of life – the gift of a child."

At all and any cost Dr Adam knew that he must do something to undo that with which he had been complicit. He had only just had the results back from the laboratory. They confirmed his worst fears. This child was a monster whose DNA was a mutant mass.

Under his careful management, the months of hormone treatments had successfully rejuvenated her fertility. Maria had relied on his ego and competitive nature – the need to succeed whatever the consequences – he had never considered her motives. She had understood him so well. Now that he understood this, Dr Adams was on his guard, she was capable of reading his mind.

Why did he not question where the sperm came from? How could he have just accepted Maria's story that it came from her dead husband? This genetically engineered mixture is part human, part arachnid. He must find out where it came from and how many more of these hybrids had been created. He said, as calmly as he could, "Of course, Maria, you are right the pregnancy is confirmed. Now we must ensure that it goes to term. Come sit on the couch and I will give you an iron injection." If I can only get this into her, Dr Adams thought, she will spontaneously abort.

Maria moved toward the couch slowly, a thoughtful look

in her cold, unblinking eyes. Suddenly, she turned and moved swiftly to the door. Dr Adam grabbed her, trying desperately to get restraints around her arms and shoulders. The struggle was short lived and violent. Dr Adam's nurse reported seeing Maria leave – she had been smiling benignly, serenely rubbing her swollen stomach and humming softly to herself.

5. The skyscrapers stretched out against the darkened horizon – some buildings broken in half, others without roofs, some sitting at rakish angles. The smoke still moved around the city in wisps. The roads were buckled, intermittently pitted with craters. In these holes it was possible to see the broken communication and electricity cables. At the corners of many streets small geysers gushed from fractured water pipes. The battle between the contaminated armies and the small pockets of un-infected individuals was finally over.

Across the airwaves came the first independent radio broadcast for nearly two years. "To all those who can hear this, please be aware that the war with CONTROL (Committee of Neurological Transformation Research Overcoming Logic) is over. The antidote to CONTROL's nerve gas should now be taking effect and many of you will be feeling disoriented. Please stay tuned for more information on where to go for medical assistance. Do not proceed to the hospitals – they are full to capacity."

Marcia turned to Gavin and said, "Thank God it's over!" Gavin's face relaxed for the first time in months, "It will be wonderful to have everyone and everything back to normal." "I know," replied Marcia, "it is hard to

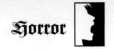

comprehend that so few of us were able to beat CONTROL, against all odds."

Out in the street, Marvin sat on a park bench in a daze, trying to remember what he had been doing for the last 24 months. How odd, he thought, before I was a musician, working alone and living in a world of free form creative angst. I never wanted to be in the military. Yet the last few months have been my happiest. I knew my place in the group and was content. I am not sure I want to go back to the old life. As the antidote continued to take effect, groups of chatting and laughing people who had been working in teams began to break up. Individuals drifted aimlessly through the rubble with dazed expressions on their faces, not speaking. They may have been coming out of their own personal hell. Or perhaps they were just entering into one? Still recovering and not sure where they were, or even who they were, not one of them seemed interested in rescuing their belongings or finding friends or family. Each was isolated – realising, perhaps for the first time how each one was very alone. The quiet sat like a blanket in the air.

Apparition	ghostly spirit that can be seen
Axe murderer	mad
Bats	associated with vampires
Blood	
Broomsticks	traditional transport for witches
Brew	to cook spells, potions
Cats	associated with witches a traditional 'familiar'
Cemetery	graveyard
Coven	a collection of witches
Cross	the symbol of Christianity – goodness used against unclean spirits
Crypt	a tomb, sarcophagus
Dark side	working for evil
Devil	also Satan, Old Harry, Old Nick, The Fallen Angel, the Dark Master, Lucifer – the embodiment of evil and the master of all sinister and evil beings.
Disembodied	body parts that are separated from the main torso (heads, hands, legs) Often still functioning – heads in jars, hands that still do jobs etc.
Druids	ancient Celtic religious cult
Dungeon	ancient prison in the cellars of castles and other fortifications. Often associated with evil events.

Effigy	a replica of an individual, often made in wax and adorned with personal effects. Traditionally used to harm the person it represents
Enchanted	under the influence of a magical spirit,
Evil	opposite of good
Evisceration	cutting open and removing the organs and guts
Familiar	animal that is associated with witches, warlocks etc.
Full moon	a phase of the moon when werewolves manifest themselves, and madness (lunacy) is more likely
Flaying	skinning alive
Garlic	traditionally wards off vampires
Genetic Engineering	branch of science that can produce unnatural living things
Ghosts	the spirits of those that have passed
Ghouls	bloodthirsty evil beings
Gore	blood, guts, viscera
Gorge	to feast and be swelled with blood (usually)
Hovels	poor, dirty dwellings often the home of witches
Madness	mental illness
Manacled chained	at wrist and ankle
Morgue	place where bodies are kept before burial

Mutilation	terrible injury to body, often involving flaying, evisceration
Paranormal	beyond normal, from the other side
Pestilence	plagues, boils, locusts, etc
Poltergeist	unruly destructive, noisy spirit
Potions	mixtures of oils and unpleasant ingredients to use in magic
Premonition	an unbidden vision of the future
Psychopath	a mentally ill killer without conscience
Ravens	large black birds that are seen to have a magical influence
Scythe	a large cutting implement, used for cutting corn, symbol of death
Second Sight	the ability to see into the future
Sinister	literally means the left side but is usually used to indicate that a person or activity is evil
Spells	incantations used to effect magical change
Stake in the heart	well known way to kill vampires
Supernatural	something greater than the normal or natural
Super race	unusually tall and strong beings, that are usually a hybrid of human with another supernatural being
Torture	deliberate infliction of extreme pain on another

Torment	a state of unbearable suffering
Trance	dazed like state where individuals can not control their own behaviour
Un-dead or Living Dead	reanimated dead people, evil
Vampires	mythical dead beings that suck the blood of humans, either killing them, or turning them into vampires
Voodoo	magical religious cult of Haiti, using curses, dolls and zombies
Warlock	male witch
Werewolf	half-man half-wolf, turning into the latter at full moon
Witch	female follower of the devil, (usually) able to perform magic
Writhe	snakelike movement, usually followed by… in agony
Zombie	re-animated corpse

FANTASY

Fantasy fiction is not new, although its transcendence of the written word into games and film leads many people to believe that it is a 20th or 21st century phenomenon. Fantasy, together with science fiction and horror, are collectively known as 'speculative fiction'. This can be loosely translated as 'What if?'

Science fiction imagines that within the bounds of scientific possibility; what if these things were to happen in the not too distant future or could have happened in the past? Horror asks what if the world we can touch and see and which we can control is not all there is? Let's suppose that there is a dark and evil underworld, in which magic, psychotic behaviour and all manner of evil exists, usually with the intention of harming us.

Fantasy takes a further leap into speculation by asking, what if other worlds have existed or do exist, at the same time as ours, but in another dimension or parallel universe, bound only by their own physical rules and conventions. Alice's Wonderland is a fantasy world; as of course is the wizarding world of J.K. Rowling's Harry Potter series and JRR Tolkein's Middle Earth in *Lord of the Rings*. The complex worlds of Phillip Pullman's *His Dark Materials* trilogy are perfect examples too. Interestingly, three out of four of these are books written ostensibly for children. As of course are *The Chronicles of Narnia*, by C.S Lewis and Terry Pratchett's *Discworld* novels.

The theory is that the capacity for children to suspend their disbelief easily and make imaginative leaps, untainted by experience, gives writers the opportunity to present and explore complex philosophical, even moral questions through allegorical narrative. However, the success of fantasy games, comics and movies, as well as Internet 'virtual worlds' like 'Second Life', suggests that the appetite for fantasy fiction, long appreciated by many readers, is equally strong amongst a wide adult audience. All of the novels above have been read avidly and enjoyed by a huge adult readership. Undoubtedly, part of the success of sites like 'Second Life', can be attributed to the fact that the 'avatars', as the adopted personas of participants are called, can interact with the imaginative creations of others. Although, it may be less collaborative to create a fantasy world on paper, you are still inviting your readers to interact with you, by using their imaginations to 'see' your characters and settings in three dimensions.

Like horror, fantasy can take the basis for its characters and narrative from the archetypes of myth, fable and legend. Fantasy fiction worlds are entirely self-sufficient and it is not necessary for the characters in your story to be physically or culturally familiar to your readers. The narrative may be informed by the exploration of various universal themes, such as good versus evil, survival in a hostile environment, love and death and so on, but good fantasy uses the opportunity to consider them from a new and original perspective, unadulterated by contemporary experience and prejudice. The central characters inhabit landscapes born entirely of the author's imaginative powers.

Within the fantasy structure, any setting, or fantastical elements, powers or locations are possible. Sometimes, fantasy worlds have portals into the real world (the wardrobe in *The Chronicles of Narnia* or the railway platform in the Harry Potter books, for example) but it is not necessary for there to be interaction at all between the real and the fantasy world. If you decide that your work demands it, you will need to devise a means for characters to enter another dimension and move between two worlds or more. In each they may have different powers or may even take a different physical form. The ageing process may be accelerated or slowed down in the fantasy world, since one of the frequent features of these other worlds is that time passes differently, in order that the potentially long absence of a character from their real world setting goes unnoticed.

If you are drawn to write fantasy, it is important to remember that all your characters must abide by the conventions that you outline for your fantasy setting, or settings, behaving according to the rules you have set, or any plotting will collapse. Each world and its elements must have limits too, so that characters can develop in testing and resisting them. Magical elements should be balanced, and their powers often come at a cost. If you assign powers to one, you must give balancing powers to another, so that conflicts can be resolved. Without these boundaries, checks and balances, there is no reason for the plot to ever reach a climax and be concluded to the reader's or your own satisfaction. Whilst the sort of detailed technical and historical research that other genres require is not essential to write fantasy, there should be an intrinsic logic in the world you devise and the actions of its characters. Beyond these constraints this world is your oyster.

It is advisable, to use both a basic plotline and a character chart before you put finger to keyboard or pen to paper, and add any additional characters and events as they occur. In a world where anything is possible, it is extremely easy to lose a few people inexplicably in the course of the book, or to fail to complete a strand of the plot, because you have lost the thread.

Fantasy plots are very often centred around quests for magical objects, which are said to confer special powers or to be of themselves essential to the saving of the world.

If you devise several different species of creature, as in *The Lord of the Rings*, for example, where elves, trolls, men, hobbits, dwarves etc all interact, it is important to pick one or two representatives of each species to develop as fully-rounded personalities. As the plot evolves, these individuals will come to represent the rest of their kind.

Therefore, they must display a range of character traits, good and bad, wise and foolish, so as to hold the reader's interest and to enable them to react predictably to actions in the narrative. These characters must be able to increase their understanding of one another, and move the plot forward. As many will be completely original, you must find ways to reveal their history and motivation. Ancient volumes containing 'gnarllore' might be discovered. Stories told around a campfire might tell of glorious exploits. One character might reveal to another that which they have heard tell of 'gnarls', and so on.

Fantasy fiction is often written in a combination of styles. Descriptive passages are interspersed with dialogue, new languages are created and often lyrical elements like songs and poetry are included. This versatility in the narrative makes this an attractive genre for the writer who wants to explore his or her own creative range. However, you do need to be disciplined about how many narrative tools you use and how often. Otherwise the reader becomes aggravated, rather like sitting in a room in which so many patterns, colours and styles have been combined that one longs for white walls and a wooden chair. Finally, of all genre, fantasy is that in which you need to be very sure that you really understand the rules in order to be able to break them.

Beginnings

1. Catherine had been walking for hours when she came upon the deep green pool. She had been trying to come to terms with the implications of all the changes that were happening in her life and to make some kind of sense of the future. David had taken the children to visit their cousins for a day or two, while he and Cathy worked through their difficulties. It wasn't that she was depressed exactly, but

she was finding it increasingly difficult to shrug off the feeling of deep foreboding that descended slowly each day when the morning rituals had been completed and her brain switched from automatic to fully engaged. Poor David seemed really worried that this was a bad sign, one deeply familiar to them both, and distinctly reminiscent of the post natal depression that she had suffered after Jemmy's birth, and which had nearly torn the family apart.

Out here in the National Park, that bordered the tiny garden of the cottage, alone with her thoughts, with the sounds of the curlews keening as they rode the thermals in the empty sky, Catherine felt far more like her old self – her real self. The air was crisp, and there was a touch of the coming autumn in the subtle changes in the light. The changing seasons were always welcome to her; she felt all the possibility of renewal in the gentle transition from one to the other. A twig snapped in the undergrowth and she caught a glimpse of a bright eye and a hastily withdrawn tail as some small creature bolted for home.

As the sun began to warm the earth beneath her feet, she let her thoughts drift and just walked for a while, luxuriating in her freedom. She was usually such a stickler for the rules of the countryside, that she surprised herself when she decided to take a diversion across the meadow to the edge of the wood, and onward to the stream, rather than sticking to the path. There it is again, she thought to herself, one of those tiny aberrations from the norm which of itself means nothing, but added to all the other tiny aberrations, is taking me further and further away from the woman I had thought myself to be.

It wasn't until she had trekked some way through the woodland that led to the stream, a river really at this time of year, swelled by the waters running down from the hills, that she noticed what could only be called a slight thickening of the light. It was as if someone had placed a giant closely-woven cobweb over the wood, diffusing rather than diminishing the light. Catherine shook her head a little and rubbed her eyes, but to no effect. She pushed her way on through a bramble patch and it was only a few paces further before she nearly stepped into the pool.

Here, the strange effect of the light intensified and seemed to shimmer for a hundredth of a second as she looked down into the water at her own worried reflection...

2. The battle had been raging for four hours now; and three times Michael had been within seconds of making it to the shimmering doorway, only for it to disappear with a sound like a broken wind-chime. Time after time, the spectral warriors had beaten him back and his powers had diminished. He was nearing exhaustion, only frustration with himself made him click the mouse again to continue the game from level five.

Sure, he should be at school, but the final exams were over, and he had not felt much like participating in senior arts week, after the break-up with Jules. He still couldn't believe that he had now to face the long vacation before he began his university degree in October, without the girl who had been so essential to him from that first night. It was at the school dance, when the coloured lights had bounced off her braces, and she had given him a smile that was literally dazzling. Yeah, they had both been only twelve, but Michael had known in an instant that she was the one.

Smart, funny and kind, Jules had grown into a gorgeous young woman. What was it that she had said as they lay slumped across his bed flicking through the TV channels to find a movie to watch? She had known for some time that she needed some space to find out who she was, without being joined at the hip to Michael. She had decided to go travelling by herself, and if she was honest, she didn't expect to walk back into their relationship when she returned. She had waited until after the exams were over to tell him. That was so like her, so considerate, he thought, with a trace of bitterness. Just what was he supposed to do, with half his soul lost, wandering around the Thai-Laos border?

He turned his attention back to the game. If he could defeat the spectral warriors, and gain their transforming power, escape through the doorway, find the skeleton key and make it to level six, he might just survive another day without her. He recharged his power belt, clicked the mouse and moved across the dungeon floor towards the doorway. The warriors appeared, as he had known they would, but this time they lay down their swords and beckoned to Michael to join them...

3. Thea watched from behind the force field as the tiny creatures battled it out on the jousting ground. The earth was scorched and in some places little pools of greenish liquid still burned, releasing wisps of curling jade smoke and the strangely corrupt smell of dargon's blood into the air. Could he possibly find the reserves of strength he would need to master Ligen's worthy champion?

Her chief advisor, Mygor had explained to her that the full-grown peoples of her kingdom has settled their disputes by dargon fight for hundreds of years. Ever since the mighty dragons had begun to diminish, mutating and evolving into these, the fiercest of their descendents, the dargons, millions of Zanton lives had been saved by battle by proxy. Although Legin was not of Zanton, it was crucial that the marriage settlement of lands and treasury gold be agreed before he could wed Thea. When the Camras council had concluded its disputation of the case, dargon duelling had been the only way to settle the final boundary issues between her people and his. This betrothal had brought the first peace between the two mighty nations that the region had seen in a hundred years or more. The marriage would seal the treaty and the long awaited new age of Zanto could begin.

Once, art and music had flourished in the maple-groved city. The people had been prosperous enough to earn the leisure needed to enjoy them. Food had been in abundance and they could not have guessed that the spring, which welled from deep in the mountain and had brought life to the region since time began, would now begin to slow, so that all that remained was a trickle, slowly filing the crystal reservoirs with pure water. It was all that ordinary Zantons could do to keep their families warm and fed. There had been no time to compose the lyrical poetry for which Zanto was rightly famed, nor to paint the brightly coloured abstract pictures that had brought wealth and prestige to the capital city's art academy. But all of this would change. Legin's lands had abundant supplies of fresh water and livestock, and it would be a simple matter to divert the mighty river Hsitnek, to flow through the border countries.

The dargon-master entered the arena now, dressed in his protective armour and the tevs examined the beasts for injury, treating any internal wounds on the touch screens attached to their wrists. The Zantons could not countenance a fight until death, so the masters would access the injuries and declare a victor. If Thea's champion had been successful, she would complete the marriage contract with Legin, and journey with him to the source of the spring and the city would rise again...

4. Tom shook his head in disbelief; one moment he had been travelling on the bus, and the next he was soaring high above the countryside. It was an exhilarating feeling. This, in itself, was extraordinary, since Tom had never cared for air travel, which was why he had chosen to cross the country by bus in the first place. But this sense of freedom and yes, joy, was nothing like sitting cramped and uncomfortable in an aircraft cabin, breathing other people's air and touching knees with a complete stranger. He was so high now he asked himself why his head had not exploded, and the speed was indescribable.

Tom turned into the warm air and attempted a small manoeuvre. To his surprise, it worked and he found that he could change direction quite easily. But where was he going? The bus, a tiny dot far, far below him seemed to be going in the opposite direction. Tom should be worried, but he was too happy to fret.

He assumed that whatever force had plucked him from his bumpy seat over the wheel arch, knew where he was going. It was difficult to imagine that any power, which could present him with this marvellous experience, could also bear him any ill will.

The euphoria lasted until the air started to chill rapidly and Tom began to lose all feeling in his fingers and toes. His teeth began to chatter and it was with some relief that he felt himself losing height. It was dusk now, and occasional lights from houses and townships blinked up at him from the ground below.

He did not seem to be slowing down however, just moving on a lower plane. He turned to the west and was soon flying into the most glorious sunset, over the shining silver ocean. He could see the race ahead as he lost still more height. The point at which the turning tides met was swirling into an ever-increasing whirlpool of foaming sea. He dipped suddenly into a dive and he could hear his own screams echoing in the quiet evening, as he nose-dived into the heart of the whirlpool.

For a moment the silence of the ocean was deafening, as he struggled against the swirling waters. "Stop struggling," a voice in his head seemed to say, "Let the water carry you." He tried a few tentative kicks against the water, at the same time undulating his body as he seen the dolphins at the sea life centre do. He began to move through the water as effortlessly as he had the air, only moments before. As he moved further from the heart of the race, the waters began to clear and it was then that he had his first glimpse of the coral city...

5. Ferdie struggled against the ropes that bound him like a cocoon from neck to ankle. He felt sick and afraid as, suspended from a pole carelessly supported on the shoulders of two of the biggest, the creatures transported him through the rain forest. He knew that he mustn't allow them to see his fear, so he kept up this pretence that he had any chance of escape. In his heart he knew that loosening the bounds was impossible. Ferdie was by nature an optimist, so he reassured himself that although he was fiendishly uncomfortable, he was probably safe enough for the moment. After all, if these things had wanted him dead, they could have killed him the moment that he walked into the pit, and indeed at any time since. Why were they keeping him alive? What did they want with him? If only he understood their language, he would be able to pick up on the conversations going on around him in harsh guttural voices.

He would have to wait until he was in slightly more auspicious circumstances to get their measure. They seemed to be sticking closely to the line of the steaming green river, and Ferdie could hear the occasional sound of something worryingly heavy and slow moving entering the water. Above him the birds shrieked with anger at the disturbance in their peace. The amulet that Narga had insisted on giving to him swung free from his shirt as they marched. Suddenly, it began to glow faintly in the green light filtering through the trees. It seemed to Fergie that he could feel a warmth rising from the clear red stone and spreading through his whole body.

He concentrated all his life energy into his eyes as he stared hard at the stone. It began to rotate infinitesimally against its setting. At the same time, Ferdie could feel it vibrating softly against his chest. His heart leapt and he tried hard to focus; fighting the pain is his constricted limbs. He must remember to concentrate on the one significant word that might activate the amulet. He had no idea whether the creatures had telepathic powers. Suddenly, his mind found the word he was searching for, Ganandra! Quickly he translated it, using the code he had been taught. Tonnunbra, Tonnunbra, he thought with all his might. The bounds began to loosen and uncoil and he pulled himself upright on the pole and with one triumphant cry, soared high above the canopy of trees, clinging for dear life to the rough pole between his knees…

Endings

1. Asterim moved quickly and silently along the darkened alley. Fortunately, he was able to avoid the open sewer running down its centre, by bending his knees and tucking his feet up under the mantle, so that he could glide just above the surface. Unfortunately, he could not avoid the miasma that rose like a presence from the ground. He wrinkled his nostrils in distaste, as the smell threatened to overwhelm him. Wrapping his kerchief around the lower part of his face anew, he continued on his way, tapping gently at each door as he passed, with the long staff he carried in his right hand. An answering tap told him that friends dwelled within, on whom he could count in the days to come.

Some houses, he knew, were occupied by lone children, orphaned by the years of bloody conflict, and some by women raising their children in the darkness, but with light in their hearts and minds, against the dawn of a new day for the kingdom. None of these had been expected to fight, but their coded knocks gave him to understand that they had played their part by forming a string of safe houses across the city, where fugitives and refugees could find some respite from the torture, and medical attention for their wounds, if need be, before continuing to the hills to join the resistance.

Under the protection of the mantle, Asterim was in no real danger himself this night, but he could feel the fear, like a palpable presence rising from the cramped streets, along with the stench.

Even though the battle had been won, and the tyrant's troops had been driven out of the city, the troops had burned and pillaged as they retreated, and the diseases borne by the rats, as they wallowed in the filth and the spoiled grain stores were already taking their toll. These people had suffered enough, and Asterim's report would recommend that they receive the magical reconstruction they had so justly earned. Although the civil war had diminished the powers of the wizards of the elite too, they could still muster enough magic between them to make reparation to these brave citizens for their terrible losses. Tragically, even the mighty Gasden, could not bring back those who had given their lives for the cause. Yet, the townsfolk had offered no recriminations, and the wizards had managed to counteract the spell of eternal night that had been cast as the last desperate act of the great tyrant before his defeat. Now, a watery sunshine began to dawn over the spires of the city and Asterim's heart lifted as he heard the sound of a single bird's song greet the dawn.

2. Ruby heard her mother calling from the kitchen and began to put the tiny people back into their respective places in the doll's house.

It was time for her to have her supper, and if she was a good girl and tidied away her toys quickly, Mummy might let her come back after supper to play a little longer with the dolls' house before her bath and bed. The tiny copper pots and pans glowed in the red paper firelight of the cosy kitchen as she set Mrs Dudley down gently before the stove. The soup was almost ready and soon she and Daisy would carry the miniature tureen up to the dining room where Ruby had already lit the lamps and laid the table for the family to have their dinner. Daisy had folded the starched white table napkins this morning and Ruby put them carefully beside each place. If only her fingers were less sausagy, she could be of more help to the little people. But she was getting too big to put the tiny infant in her cot, or bath the twins in the claw foot cast iron bath in the nursery bathroom.

She left the big-hinged front of the house a little ajar as she stood up to leave the room. That way, the family would know that she would be coming back after her own meal. Clare smiled at her little daughter as she sat up at the kitchen table and gave her a quick hug. Ruby had played so quietly with the dolls' house all afternoon, that Clare was able to finish sewing the latest consignment of children's clothes and parcel them up ready to be posted, while Emerald took her afternoon nap. The rosy toddler was sitting in her high chair now, smiling gummily at Ruby, who she adored. Ruby held Emmie's little hand and the baby laughed as her big sister played round and round the garden in her little palm.

Still Ruby was not completely untroubled, as tomorrow was the day she was to start at proper school and she was worried about what would happen to the little family in the dolls' house while she was away all day. Emmie gazed at her big sister and laughed again. She was such a cheerful little thing that it was hard for Ruby to stay anxious for long. She had seen the family through the very difficult times and somehow Daisy and Mrs Dudley would just have to manage without her. Suddenly Emmie opened her mouth and looking straight at Ruby, said "I'll take care of them Ruby." Surely Mum must have heard that thought Ruby, she had been waiting for weeks for Emmie to extend her vocabulary beyond mama, dad, Ru and me. But Clare didn't seem to have heard Emmie speak. Ruby felt much happier, she hadn't known if her little sister would understand about the little people, but now she realised that although she might be getting bigger, Emmie's little fingers were just the right size for the dolls' house and there would always be someone to take care of them and protect them from the others.

3. The ship had been becalmed for several days now and the crew was becoming restless. The captain raised his telescope to his eye, hoping to catch movement in the cloud formation that would indicate a change in the wind. Jack Cranham was in the crow's nest scanning the horizon for any sign of land. The first mate, Abel Jones, stood beside the captain but said nothing. Only he knew what this last voyage had cost the captain and he felt his skipper's unspoken pain and anxiety as if it were his own. After overcoming so much, could he yet fail to bring his ship and her crew safely home? A soft zephyr brushed the captain's face, and the cloud that covered the sun moved a little to let a shaft illuminate his careworn features. The golden light lifted the skipper's spirits for a moment and he half-smiled, softening the craggy features and hard lines of his face.

Below decks, the timbers creaked ominously as their cargo shifted in the hold. The captain's smile disappeared as rapidly as it had come, leaving not a ghost of it on his shadowed face. He would ask no man to go below and check the hold. There was not one who would not go unbidden, but he couldn't bring himself to let good men risk their very souls. Wearily, he handed over the bridge to the mate and made his way down to the hold. The thick oak doors were barred with strong iron cross bars and the bolts were reinforced with iron bolts, fashioned at their last port of call. The captain was fairly confident that the doors would hold, but he knew that if the monster within had caught wind of the fact that they were becalmed, he would use every ounce of his immense power to batter the doors and escape, or sink the ship in the attempt. The captain didn't often pray but he muttered a quiet request to the gods of the sea to keep faith with him a little longer.

The ship rocked gently, and the captain uttered a word of thanks. The wind was getting up and he could hear the shouted orders above decks and the sound of crew making ready to go about, as soon as the wind gathered strength. If he could only get the ship into the channel for home and then turn her rapidly all might still be well. It had been a condition of their negotiated departure from that other sea, in that other dimension, under different stars, that they take aboard this fearful burden and not release it until they reached the offing of their own land. The captain peered into the hold, through the specially constructed spy hole and the cargo seemed steady enough.

Returning to the bridge he waited for the optimum moment and gave the order to turn for home. The crew gave a muted, "Hurrah!" and the faithful vessel turned. Now, they had the wind in her sails and would make good speed. The boy in the crow's nest called "Land ho," and the captain gave the order to go about again.

The ship seemed as anxious as the crew to help her master and they managed the manoeuvre perfectly, just as they reached shallower water. The captain ordered the crew to cover their eyes and touched the centre of the wheel, as he had been instructed to do. The bow of the ship seemed to dissolve, revealing the horror within. With a mighty roar the dark shape moved into the water, causing the swell to rise up over the deck. For a moment, it seemed to pause and swim and then with a flash of white light, it disappeared and the bow of the ship reformed.

This time the crew's 'hurrahs' were deafening as the ship turned about a third time, and headed for home. The captain's smile outshone the sun that warmed his heart as they headed towards the port and the arms of their wives and sweethearts - at last.

4. It would never be over, never be finished, completed, and fulfilled. This terrible pact, which demanded that she give more and more of her very soul every day. Four years ago, Virginia Drew had given her word to Bargoth that she would stay to see the offspring fledged and flying the nest. She was not their mother, nor even a surrogate, but this had been the price of her own child's life and safe return to their own London and her father. Virginia was tempted every day to break that promise, to use the portal that appeared at the same time each night at the very doors of Westminster Abbey. Charlotte had been a babe in arms when Virginia had wrapped her in a gossamer shawl and laid her in the box on the steps of the great cathedral. She had managed to send a messenger earlier with the instructions to Francis to collect her on the other side. She had stood and watched as the portal opened and the baby disappeared and she had wept then and every day since.

The females had all fled the city as soon as the fledglings began to tap inside their giant shells. They would not harm Bargoth, he was their past and their future, but they would consume every other of their kind before flying out of the dimension to find mates in some other zone. Bargoth had not told her that it would take so long for the hideous birds to reach maturity and release her from her promise, and she ached for home, her husband and her child.

Bargoth would not renege on his promise. The woman could leave. He respected Virginia for her honour and he knew that she was in the most excruciating spiritual pain at the loss of her family. He allowed her to watch them through the windows of the church, as Charlotte took her first steps, said her first words and luxuriated in the undivided attention of her loving father. When Virginia returned home, it would be hard for the little girl to share him, even with her beautiful and loving mother.

The fledglings gathered on the bridge, preening themselves and admiring their own and one another's fine new feathers and razor sharp beaks of blue and yellow. Virginia whistled softly and crooned to the fledglings and they turned their black eyes toward her. She was the mother. Bargoth gave the signal and Virginia walked out onto the bridge and led the birds to the rail. In turn, each of the six hopped up and perched there waiting for instructions. Virginia climbed up onto the rail and spread her arms wide. Closing her eyes, she crooned to the birds again. Each spread its wings wide and waited. She opened her eyes and looked up at the great clock, waiting for it to strike the hour.

Bargoth bowed to her reverentially, and the clock began to chime the hour. Virginia leaped off the rail and the fledglings followed suit. Then, as the last chime rang out, she turned away from the water and flew towards the open portal. The fledglings flew on into the dying sun and one by one disappeared into envelopes of sky and onward to their new life. Virginia heard the last dying echo of the bells as she ran into the arms of her husband and precious little daughter.

5. The elves laughed their silvery tinkly laughs and watched as Hugh struggled through the metamorphosis that turned him from an average sized man to someone small enough to walk amongst the elves. He hated the process; firstly drinking the endless tiny cups of potion that they brought to him, and then the painful changes in his body as he reformed elf-side, as it were.

This was to be his last trip, he was getting too old to be rearranged every couple of months and he wanted to settle down with Alicia and start a family. He had good friends amongst the elves and he did not resent their laughter, he enjoyed listening to their light voices and watching their quicksilver ways.

Not many agents were chosen for so delicate a mission and he had been both honoured and pleased to lead this mission for the past ten years.

The elves were too honourable and proud to spy, but as they moved between the worlds so freely, they picked up a lot of useful information and could be persuaded to share it with someone who they trusted and respected. Two wars had been averted home-side as a result of elvish intelligence, and Hugh/Heramos was very proud to have been a part of inter-world events. He preferred the designer clothes and comfortable shoes he wore at home, to the tights and pointed shoes that represented the height of elfish fashion, but he needed to blend in. As it was the boffins had never managed to make him quite as tiny as the others, so he loomed rather over the elf helping him to button his boots. Still, he could pass as a tall cousin.

He met with Sandalmar in the oak office of the elfish homeland department and handed over his papers. One last report and he was bound for Civvy Street and life as a family man. The distinguished elder invited him to sit and poured a glass of the ruby red cordial that made Heramos feel so much better after a transformation. He had now left Hugh behind and was wholly Heramos, most loyal subject of the king. Sandalmar congratulated him on this, his last mission, and invited him to surrender his sword.

Reluctantly, he laid the weapon on the velvet cushion and watched as it became no longer a weapon but a symbol of his willingness to fight if his country needed him. Sandalmar raised him up and presented him with a tiny key and said that he hoped that Heramos and the lovely Alicia would be very happy in their new home. Heramos left the ministry as quickly as was polite. Who would have thought it? He, Hugo Franklin-Hotspur, elf for life.

Abyss	deep bottomless chasm
Apparitions	things that appear, ghosts
Auger	someone or something that tells the future
Charms	protections or spells
Chasm	a deep fissure
Chimera	a female fire-breathing monster in Greek mythology, typically with a lion's head on a goat's body with a serpent's tail. Can be any mismatched monster
Cloaked	hidden
Code	a system of letters and numbers or symbols, into which normal language can be translated to transfer information in secret
Conflict	disagreement
Cryptic	hidden by code
Darkness	the opposite of light, represents evil
Distopia	a society, which is unhappy and dysfunctional
Distortion	altered from the norm
Dodo	large extinct bird
Domination	power or control over others
Dragon	mythical, fire-breathing, giant, winged, scaled creatures
Dream	unconscious series of images that pass through the mind
Dwarves	mythical, small, magical, man-like creatures associated with mountains, mines and buried treasure, sometimes malevolent
Elect the	the chosen ones
Elements	parts of, specifically air, fire, earth, water
Elves	fairy-like mischievous magical creatures
Evil	opposite of good

172

Fear	an unpleasant feeling of apprehension and distress at the closeness of danger
Geomancy	a prophesy from a pattern made when earth is thrown down or dots drawn at random or connected with lines
Ghasts	ghostly apparitions
Giants	huge, mythical creatures, not often very bright
Glimmer	A slight light, or vague idea
Gorgon	a monstrous, mythical woman with snakes for hair who turned those who looked at her to stone (Greek)
Griffin	a mythical creature with the head and wings of an eagle and the body of a lion
Guide	someone who leads through portals or mysteries
Hierarchy	an order, usually social, with the lowest at the bottom and the highest at the top
Hobgoblin	a mythical mischievous usually malevolent creature
Illusion	something imagined that turns out not to be real
Imperceptible	unable to be perceived
Incantation	a spoken spell, used repetitively
Innocent	pure, untainted
Journey	travel with a particular purpose
Justice	fairness, especially in the way that people are treated and decisions are made.
Magic	a special, mysterious property or skill
Magical objects	items that can be imbued with special qualities or powers
Manifestation	physical representation

Mantle	cloak
Mask	disguise
Materialise	to make physically substantial
Messengers	those who take messages between places or people
Metamorphosis	complete transforming change
Miasma	a harmful or poisonous emanation, especially from decaying or organic matter
Mirage	a vision
Morphing	changing
Mortality	the ability to die
Mystery	something unexplained
Necromancy	black arts
Ogre	see giant
Oracle	foretells the future
Orc	a mythical, ugly, man-like creature usually war-like and dim-witted
Perturbation	the result of being troubled and worried
Phantasm	a ghostly manifestation
Phenomenon	something extraordinary and unique
Portal	gateway or doorway
Precipice	a sharp drop from a cliff
Prism	a transparent polygonal solid object with flat faces and a usually triangular cross section, through which white light separates into colours
Protection	A means of defence
Quest	A journey in search of a particular object or place

Rainbow	the multicoloured formation which appears in the sky after rain
Rebellion	the result of rising up against rules or authority
Refraction	the change in direction that occurs when a wave of energy such as light passes from one medium to another of a different density, for example, from air to water
Rubric	a set of directions for conduct
Runes	ancient markings and symbols which bear a hidden meaning
Seer	someone who can see what is hidden, such as the future
Symbols	something which stands instead of something else
Telepathy	thought transference and the ability to read minds
Totem	a symbol bearing magical or cultural significance
Transformation	complete change
Trepidation	anxiety and fear
Trolls	see orcs (slightly smaller than)
Utopia	an ideal world
Veil	a transparent curtain behind which something is hidden
Visions	something seen with the mind's eye
Weapons	items used against others to wound, injure or kill either in defence or offence

175

THRILLER/ACTION ADVENTURE

How is a thriller defined, and how does it differ from some aspects of crime, horror or even science fiction? There is a considerable degree of overlap these days. It is certainly possible to write a horror thriller, or a crime thriller or a romantic thriller, as long as it includes a good dose of adrenalin pumping suspense, in short, thrills. But each of those have other criteria to fulfil, which define their genre, whereas here, we are concerned with a straightforward story which has us on the edge of our seat and which we cannot put down until we have finished it. That does not mean that the plot and characterisation is not complex.

Characteristically, thrillers have been plot driven, rather than character driven in the sense that many deal with large world-threatening plots, foreign powers or individuals who wish to bring the planet to its metaphorical knees. The plot of the novel cannot reach its climax until the sinister power is unmasked and his or their evil plans are foiled. In this sense there is no mystery, or crook to be found, as in a crime novel, or perpetrator of a single crime who must be brought to justice. There are of course exceptions such as the determined and elusive serial killer. Normally, the lone hero knows who is responsible and is dedicated to stopping them at all costs, rather than bringing them to justice.

You will need to supply your reader with a fair degree of large scale violence of the blowing things up kind, if you want to write a traditional thriller, as well as high technological and political content, plenty of cunning gadgets and high speed chases involving expensive motorbikes, motorcars, and aeroplanes. Your hero will normally be in mortal peril during the greater part of the book. Although, notably short on high-tech devices, John Buchan's *The*

Thirty Nine Steps is the quintessential early modern thriller, in which the unfortunate, but resourceful Richard Hannay, becomes involved in a foiling an enemy plot and finds himself pursued to Scotland and back, by both the police and the enemy spies, when he is falsely accused of murder.

There are exceptions to the plot driven thriller. Ian Fleming's James Bond novels, featuring the dashing secret service agent are character driven. They would not be the same if they featured the exploits and adventures of a series of different double O agents. However most thrillers do not start out as serial thrillers. The success of a hero in one title leads to his featuring in another and they only appear to be a series in retrospect. It's a good trick if you can pull it off.

As with so much popular fiction there are many sub genres of thriller. Ian Fleming's James Bond and Robert Ludlum's *Bourne Identity* for example, are typically categorised as spy thrillers, in that their heroes are government agents who are pitted against the agents of foreign powers or terrorist groups. Political thrillers usually give their heroes the grave responsibility of maintaining the stability of the government that employs them. Frederick Forsyth's *The Day of the Jackal* would be perfect example. Military thrillers feature serving officers in the armed services, doing extraordinarily brave deeds to protect the countries they serve. Conspiracy thrillers involve a maverick hero who is forced to uncover a plot, which has been hatched by the rich and powerful and may involve his own government. He often has to persuade others that his convictions are real, and he will almost certainly become an outcast as a result. Michael Crichton and Tom Clancy have been called the fathers of the Techno-thriller, which will feature a detailed knowledge of technology, which is essential to take the plot to a satisfactory conclusion.

Space does not allow a detailed analysis of every aspect of the thriller, but the psychological thriller should be considered if you prefer your suspense to be of the emotional or mental kind. Patricia Highsmith is a doyenne of the psychological thriller and if you are looking forward to selling the film rights in your work, you might consider that this is a good avenue to explore. Disaster thrillers, involving flood, volcanoes, earthquakes and nuclear disasters are also very popular with filmmakers. A relatively recent extension of disaster thrillers might be considered the eco-thriller, in which the hero represents us all, in battling governments or big business interests in order to avert a biological or environmental disaster. Wilbur Smith's *Elephant Song* is a perfect example. John Grisham is considered the master of the legal thriller and Thomas Harris leads the way in forensic thrillers. War stories and adventure on the high seas also present opportunities for courageous heroes to prove their mettle and are avidly sought by their fans. Almost all heroes of any sub genre of thriller are risking their lives and often those of others, rather than their jobs or reputations when they embark on their adventure. The bywords of the thriller might be 'lone hero or heroine' and 'writ large'.

As a writer you will need to develop a keen sense of pace and be prepared to both think big and pay attention to the fine detail. Maintaining tension over a long period involves careful plotting. It is very easy to lose track of the cause and effect of the action, when your characters are very mobile, so a plotline can be very useful here. High action content is not enough, even high octane thrills and spills pall, if they are not underpinned by tight plotting.

As ever, research is vital if you are to convince your readers that your story is credible. You will need to be certain that the travel feats that your international hero is performing are possible, and you may need to consult airline timetables and routes, international time zones, and be sure that the names and technical specifications of weapons and vehicles are accurate. Of course, you can write much smaller scale suspense thrillers in which the action takes place closer to home; Tess Gerritson's, very successful medical thrillers fall into that category. You will also have to be prepared to consider bringing your heroes to a sticky end, if the plot calls for it. This is real do or die stuff and if you place your hero in circumstances where there is real risk to his life and he is prepared to take it, you must be brave enough to follow through if necessary.

For inspiration, internet conspiracy theory sites are good sources for thriller plots, but you can also do worse than to read the newspapers from cover to cover to find a plot line on which to build your page turner.

Beginnings

1. The rain started at five thirteen and it was relentless. He had checked his watch because, that morning, there was nothing else to do. It had been five hours. Five hours in that bloody tent, five hours of a screeching owl, and that bloodcurdling screaming fox and the wait for the sound they did not want; one of Siebold's goons stumbling out of the forest and - the one sound they did want. The sound that did not come. The sound that was now 42 minutes overdue. Adams stared out across the field, at the derelict hut, roof caving in, the carved up track, the overgrown hedgerows. Nothing had happened here on this God-forsaken slice of land since the Berlin Wall came down. He had been here - west of the Bialowieza Forest - before, on that winter day in 1982, just before Andropov died, before glasnost, before oligarchs, before wise guys from Siberia bought up football teams.

Today it was dawn. The water was pouring off the trees, rivulets cascaded down the ancient Bundeswehr Zelt-Tarnmuster pattern issue tent, unerringly targeting the back of his neck. Then it had been late on a cold day, late in the cold war, and Grete shivering, had tugged her riding coat closer to her, her breath, misty in the frosty air. Today water dripped down his spine. And Grete was six foot under in Gniezno. When the Wall's concrete, graffitied slabs were consigned to the West's galleries and town squares, he should have been sent the same way, he thought. He had been a kid back in 82, now he was just another bloody museum piece. Schebitz edged forwards on his elbows, out of the tent. He swung the Heckler & Koch G36/7A3 over his shoulder, sat up and spat into the grass. "Well," he said. "At least this is easier than that AK47 of yours." "What are you doing?" "I can hear it," said Schebitz.

He listened. Nothing, just the rainfall. And then it was there, Allison C20R engine, the sound that meant that the beaten-up clapped out, dependable Bell helicopter was going to land, and magic-carpet them out of rain, wet leaves and death deferred and, via that surely deserved Maybach limousine into the Kempinski Hotel Budapest, suites 73 and 74, and Marta. The Bell was there. Coming in low, maybe too low over the trees, scattering leaves, Christ so noisy, enough to wake the dead and there were plenty of those in this blood-soaked landscape. Not too low, its skids hit the grass he was up and running, clutching the Browning L9A1.

Schebitz was just ahead, almost under the helicopter blades when he spun round. "Watch out, those bastards," he said like he was talking to himself, took the Heckler & Koch to his shoulder and sprayed the edge of the forest. Come on Schebitz, Adams screamed at the German, no bloody time but turned anyway and clutched his hands round the butt of the Browning, searching for the line. It's bloody Siebold, the bastard has finally shown himself. Schebitz screamed for point three of a second. then the Veresk sub-machine gun turned him into buzzard food. Adams fired four shots, and Siebold and five, maybe six others, were still moving, slowly, carefully, relentlessly, out of the forest...

2. She lay in bed with her eyes closed, breathing slowly, listening to her mother moving around downstairs. Another hour, she thought, another hour and I've got to get out of here. I've got to sort this out. The stairs creaked as her mother came up to kiss her goodnight. "Sleep tight, darling, sweet dreams." Her mother dropped a kiss on her forehead and she murmured in response, as her mother tiptoed away in an irritatingly exaggerated fashion, and closed the door softly behind her.

When the house was quiet, Gay got up. She had been going out at night for about a year now, and never been caught. From the backpack that she took to school she retrieved a pair of footless tights and a tight, sleeveless, black top that clung to her thighs. Hightop trainers completed her outfit. She had been stashing the items she would need for the night's work into the backpack during the last couple of days – her mother's trowel, a pair of scissors, a pen-knife, a roll of duck tape, thin nylon gloves and some neatly folded plastic sheeting. At the bottom of the backpack, wrapped in bubble wrap, was The Problem.

The bedroom window slid open silently, and as she turned to climb out, her eyes automatically checked the room. Her mother rarely woke during the night, and even if she did, why would she check on Gay? And even if she did check on Gay, she'd only peek through a crack and she'd see an arrangement that looked a lot like a sleeping daughter, safe in her bed. She closed the window behind her, crossed the flat roof of the kitchen extension, lowered herself carefully onto the water butt below and then to the ground. Walking softly around the side of the house, she reached the street, and set off towards the town.

As she walked, Gay wondered what he'd do when he realised it was missing. In fact it was all she could think about since she'd found it and this mad plan had burst fully formed into her mind. She couldn't imagine what had prompted her to just take it. Did she want him to notice her; to approve of her; like her? If so, this surely wasn't the way – this was secret and had to stay secret whatever happened. She wondered if she was right about what she thought he'd done. Of course she couldn't stop now, she had to finish her self-appointed task. She had thought of a hundred different possibilities, but this seemed to her to be the safest way to get rid of it, this Problem that seemed to be burning a hole in her back as she carried it to what would be its final resting place...

3. At first Jim McGuire had thought the guys in 'Disclose'were crazy. Lunatic conspiracy theorists, who had nothing better to do, than convince themselves that Elvis was still alive or Marilyn Monroe had been whacked by the government. Then he noticed a tiny contribution to the chat room that struck a chord.

Jim had worked in the department for five years, and he wouldn't have missed a moment of it. He had been brought up in the mid-west by good God-fearing parents, who went to church on Sundays and said grace before meals. They weren't teetotal, and though they gave money to their local church, they had never been drawn to revival tents or TV evangelists. They had worked hard, and been proud of Jim's achievements, especially when he got into Harvard. Jim was a credit to them. He loved his country, his family and his girl, and though he wasn't a churchgoer, he still conversed with the Almighty on a regular basis. He had graduated top in his class and had been pleased and flattered when the government had recruited him for the elite CIA department.

He was fit and healthy, intelligent and well balanced, with only a slight tendency to obsessive-compulsive behaviour. He liked his socks in matched pairs and his suits and pants hung up in the closet in order of shade of grey. His appraisals described him as likeable, a team player, sharply intelligent, but with a good dose of gumption thrown in. He was the perfect candidate, and so he had proved to be. That is until he had accidentally stumbled across the Sidex file, when the intern had sent up the wrong info. Initially, he thought it was just another investigation that had hit a brick wall through lack of hard-evidence, but then he had been asked to look into the Duteque problem, and because he was blessed with a photographic memory, one or two names caught his attention.

The same officers had been assigned to both investigations, and yet their reports made no mention of the similarities in the products under scrutiny, nor of the fact that the two companies had a CEO and five directors in common. His interest was piqued; he recalled the distinctive red and green sacks of fertiliser, bearing the Sidex brand, stacked up in his father's barn, from when he was a kid, and he had noticed that Duteque figured in his pa's accounts when he ran over them on his behalf before he submitted his returns to the IRS. Someone had been sloppy with this investigation. Jim clicked on the directors' names and cross-referenced them to other directorships, both at home and abroad. With no particular aim in mind, he looked down the classified files in his department's cold case files. More than half the companies had been under investigation in the past ten years, yet all had drawn a blank. He cross-referenced the teams who had investigated. This time he came up with a one hundred percent match. Something wasn't right here…

4. Katya tipped the contents of her purse out onto the dresser and felt around the inside of the zipper. She extracted a long, thin wire

from the seam and placed it next to the tiny piece of 'gum' she had unwrapped earlier. She pulled a loose thread from the button on her shirt cuff and quickly fashioned the device, just as the tech boys had shown her. She was surprised to find adrenalin pumping through her veins. Her fingers felt slippery with sweat as she set up the explosion. The door opened with a satisfactory pop and she looked out into the corridor outside. There appeared to be no guards, but the hallway thrummed with the kind of low level sound that only a lot of very expensive high tech surveillance equipment created. She had spotted the CCTV cameras on her way in, and the goon who had brought her here had gained access with retinal recognition technology. She wasn't trying to get in though, but out, so she made her way slowly down the corridor. She timed her runs to avoid the sweep of the camera, keeping close to the wall, willing herself to be patient, not to follow her instinct to get the hell out of here as fast as possible. She paused to control her breathing, her breath was coming in shallow bursts, a typical reaction to stress, or so the training manual had said. It was deeply claustrophobic, in this underground place, with the low metal ceilings and no natural light or air. Katya had worked hard to overcome that particular phobia after her experience in Bosnia in the 90s. She had been successful, but it was always there, at the back of her mind, the fear of becoming trapped in a confined space.

She had reached about halfway up the length of the corridor now, and it narrowed here, in every dimension. Katya dropped silently to the floor and rolled down towards the circular vault door at the end. Good, there was no id pad on the door, just a simple numerical code pad. She allowed herself a smile; numbers were her thing. She copied the arrangement of numbers on the pad into the palm computer keypad contained in her glove, then added some code words that might unlock a sequence. The tiny digits started computing immediately and came up with a dozen possibilities. She decided to use her very unscientific intuition and guessed. Okay, so that didn't work. She punched in her second choice and Bingo; the deadbolts drew back. Three men stood on the other side, their faces grim as they moved towards her. Katya adopted the classic defence stand and waited. "Well, Agent X," said the tall distinguished looking one in the sharp grey suit, the timing was perfect, but you relied too much on intuition. If this had not been an exercise the outcome might not have been so happy"…

5. Lady Hermione gave the impossibly handsome young man at the next table what she hoped was a flirtatious smile. She placed the Sobranie cigarette in the long holder without ever once talking her eyes from his. A waiter appeared silently at her elbow and lit it discreetly. She knew that her profile showed to best advantage in the glow of the match. Her silky black bob framed her elfin features and she closed her eyes, showing long, silky lashes against her pale cheek as she inhaled deeply.

James had described the young man perfectly, and she had readily agreed to do her best to engage him here in the bar, whilst her brother conducted a search of the young man's room. Mummy would be furious if she discovered that James had involved his sister in another of these capers. Surely, the men could win the war without putting gently nurtured females in danger. But Hermione thrived on danger; indeed she had always been the more recklessly adventurous of the twins, heedless of her personal safety, emotional and physical.

Secretly, the Colonel wished it could have been Lady Hermione that he had recruited to the service, rather than Lord James; she had more of a feel for the game. Still, it would be a black day when England depended upon its womenfolk to do the dirty work, let alone Lady Hermione Featherstone. Besides, where young

Featherstone went, Lady Hermione would be sure to follow and darned useful she had been too in the last show.

Hermione crossed her long legs, allowing just a glimpse of silk stocking top as she did so. Any moment now the young man would send a waiter with his card, she was certain. She watched under her eyelashes as he took out his card case and a silver pencil and removing a card, wrote something on the back and beckoned to the waiter. Moments later the waiter was at her elbow again, offering the salver to her with a card face downwards upon it.

Hermione had the grace to feel a moment's qualm as she accepted the card. It really wouldn't do if anyone of her acquaintance were to see her shamelessly picking up young men in seedy hotel bars. She ran through her possible aliases for when the inevitable introduction must be made, and reminded herself of the fictitious background she must use to safeguard her identity.

In the shabby hotel room on the second floor, James was making a thorough and professional job of searching the young man's belongings. From the look of the devil it wouldn't have surprised him to find a weapon or two in the battered portmanteau on top of the flimsy wardrobe. To his disappointment, he found only a bundle of papers, hastily tied with blue ribbon. As he riffled through them, his bile rose and his knuckles whitened. Good grief, the blighter had somehow managed to steal the plans for new monoplane that was causing such a stir in the corridors of Whitehall, doubtless planning to pass them on to his contact in Berlin. Damned Traitor, James had a good mind to go down stairs now and teach the little coward a thing or two about patriotism. He tucked the papers into his evening coat and made for the door, when he was halted by a sound from the corridor.

Could that be that his sister's legendary tinkling laugh coming from the hall?…

Endings

1. "Good evening, this is Marcia Adams bringing you the NVOX news at 10 o'clock. Tonight's main headlines: Carl Ferman, chairman of Ferrito inc, tonight told reporters that he had been unaware of the undisclosed health risks posed by his organisation's bio-medical research and development programme in Central Africa. He announced that he had every intention of appealing against the landmark ruling delivered today in the High Court in favour of the environmental activists Friends of Gaia.

The judge, Lord George Fortescue, ruled that the Ferrito plant, which occupies over 200 kilometres of fertile land in Central Africa, should be closed down immediately and that manufacture of the drug Feloxitane, should cease in all of the company's twelve plants worldwide. He also ruled that the cost of decontamination of the two hundred kilometre area of Gnobo, the small African State where the raw material for Feloxitane was cultivated, should be borne by Ferrito. This, together with the compensation to workers for loss of earnings is expected to run into billions. Lord Fortescue also warned Ferrito that they should prepare themselves for a series of class actions around the world for compensation to volunteers who had been inadequately prepared and misled about the drug trials in which they were participating. Lord Fortescue, said that he had never heard of a case where profits had been so deliberately and callously pursued at the expense of millions of lives."

Sarah turned off the television and clicked on the mouse to turn on her laptop. E-mails were flooding in from all over the world, rejoicing in the success of the operation. She felt exhilarated, but exhausted and tomorrow she would read them properly and answer as many as she could. Of course, it was early days yet; Ferrito might still wriggle out of their responsibilities, as the war continued to rage through the courts, but at least, the poison that they peddled would be destroyed.

What had started as a small demonstration against the exploitation of cheap labour in a developing country had become a war against one of the most powerful global capitalists in the world. She looked at the smiling faces on her screensaver. A group of young men and women, with homemade banners, protesting outside Ferrito headquarters more than five years before, and the tears came once more. Three of the five had given their lives in this war, and she and Edward might not live to see the battle won, but for the time being, the human tragedy had been averted, and that was a fitting tribute to the passionate and committed young people who were no longer here to share the victory. She logged out and clicked the remote, to see the last images of the cheering Gnobons, before saving the newly opened files on Ferrito's hidden sister company Heralde, and turning out the lights.

2. When he had first heard the tapping, he had thought that it was his captors, returning for the first time in twenty-four hours, this time to fulfill their threat to shoot him in the dust. As a journalist, he had been fully aware of the risks that he was running, remaining in this war torn country when all his colleagues had left with the last wave of withdrawing troops. Perhaps arrogantly, he had believed that he could still help the tiny emerging nation to deliver its message to the world and to initiate talks on an aid package that would 'kick start', as the papers would have it, the nascent economy.

Naturally, he had been aware that there were still pockets of resistance in the hills and that the sporadic but fierce fighting between the insurgents and the government troops would continue for months, if not years. In fact, that had been the main thrust of his reports for HDOX in the past weeks. He believed that it was too soon for troops to pull out and leave the depleted government forces to stabilize the country.

Evidently, his captors thought so too, and had imagined that the kidnap of one grumpy journo would persuade the west to stay put.

When it had become abundantly clear that this was not going to have the desired effect, they had been left with him a captive, and no way to send him back without losing face. Lying in his own filth in the coffin sized hole he had called home, he had tried to imagine the complex negotiations that might yet see him free. He knew that he had good friends on both sides of the divide and that they would not give up hope of his safe release. But it was hard to remain sane, let alone upbeat in close captivity.

Now as he faced the battery of flashing bulbs as the world's press crushed themselves against the hastily elected barriers to see and photograph the emaciated, bearded, and bewildered old man, who had once been a leading investigative reporter, he tried to smile, and to find the words they needed to hear about his relief and gratitude. Later they would want to hear that his captors had tortured and tormented him, but for now they wanted, as did he, to rejoice in his safe release. There would be time enough to tell the real and extraordinary story of his months in captivity when he got home.

3. The white fog that had engulfed him seemed to be lifting and he could just make out the shapes circled around his bed. As each formed into a more distinct and familiar pattern, his brain started to make connections again. The man holding his eyelid up and shining a bright light into first one, and then the other eye must be a doctor, because that was what doctors did. The beeping and whirring sounds were not the futile attempts of extra-terrestrials to communicate with him, but the machines that had kept him alive, breathing for him and pumping his blood around his enfeebled body.

He tried to speak, to let them know that he was back, but the words seemed to dissolve between the thought and his lips and he half-drifted back into the fog.

When they had pulled him from the water, he had been more dead than alive. His last clear memory was of the violent explosion that had ripped open the side of the dam and the terrifying sight of millions of gallons of angry water rushing through every crack and fissure; ready to carry away every last trace of the township that had grown up in its service. His unconscious had been trying to make sense of the bodies that had bumped up against him as he lay clinging to the mangled metal of a support strut. Bloated and horrific, some had been missing arms and legs; others displayed the gaping holes in their flesh where the explosion had ripped through the bone, and muscle. He wanted to ask about Mary and the kids. He prayed that they and the other townsfolk he had tried to ferry to the safety of the mountain had remained until the rescue teams could reach them. If they had tried to return for precious valuables, or lost pets, they too would have been engulfed in the raging torrent from the ruptured flood defences. He had been too late to defuse the explosives, but just in time to take out at least two of the bastards who had set them. He hoped that the fact that he was still here meant that the troops had caught the rest of the terrorist cell who had killed and maimed and devastated, to make a point. Would they never learn?

4. May 23rd 2007

I find it hard to believe that I have been in this shack in the hills for twelve months now and that no one has tried to find me. Of course, I know that is nonsense, you will have been tirelessly, searching, harrying the authorities, making television appeals.

My picture will have appeared on a million milk cartons and on

TV screens worldwide, at least at the start. Now most people, good hearted though they are, will have forgotten me, expecting only to hear someday that my body has been discovered in a shallow grave. I'm so sorry my darling, the public will be robbed of the man hunt to find my brutal killers, and you will be robbed of the justice that will allow you closure, since I cannot provide the shallow grave.

Perhaps my remains will never be found. I have tried to surround myself with lasting artifacts that will help to identify me, if anyone ever does get this far. This journal will only last a short while, I know, but the power failed before I could complete my last testament on CD and I hope that wrapped in the oilcloth, and placed in the tin box, it will remain for long enough to warn those who might come after.

Even now, I am too private a man to tell you on paper, all that is in my heart. What we have shared is too precious and too intimate to be read by strangers. Know that I love you, my dearest and that my certainty of your love for me and my knowledge of your strength and incorruptible integrity have sustained me as the inevitable decline has accelerated. I am thankful that you cannot see me, though my longing to look once more at your beautiful face and hold you in my arms is almost as excruciating as the pain of my own decay.

By now you will have found my report on the last days of the trials, and you will know that I destroyed the formula before leaving. But if I could find it, so will other minds far more brilliant than mine. This horror must never be unleashed upon the world, though in the short term it might benefit the many. I made a mistake; science cannot be of service to the world without a moral context that can never be destroyed. We both know that the corruption of power and greed means that my discovery would inevitably be used to kill as well as to cure. Still, even now, I cannot help but record the effects of the last dose of the formula. Though the decline is slow, it is remorseless. It first affects the extremities and then the vital organs. Last of all the brain begins to disconnect and the personality fragment. My other notebook describes this in scientific form, but I wanted you to know that I have managed to save enough of myself to offer you this final token of my deep love for you. I couldn't remain to infect first you and the children, and then the world with this plague. I am dying now, and it cannot be long.

Goodbye my love, until we meet in the next world. Alex.

5. The sound of rocket fire was remorseless, tearing the night sky with noise and light, like a grotesque firework display. In the bunker, Wright and Jones did not expect to get away with their lives. Around them the remains of the platoon lay scattered and torn by bullet and mortar. Wright was clinging to the gun and looking from side to side, as if in this scale of carnage, a single sniper might appear from behind the crumbling walls and look him in the eye before shooting him dead. Wright would have liked that, the personal touch, a cold bullet in this irresponsible mayhem of hot, smart weapons. He had long since lost his mind, but his soldier's training remained; keeping him focused on the prime directive, kill or be killed.

Jones was propped up against the sandbags, half his face blown away, but still conscious, poor devil. Wright would remain to protect his comrade until his last breath and he would live to fight another bloody war, on another God-forsaken battlefield, another day. Wright's loyalty would not be in vain, Jones would also survive and with reconstructive surgery, his wife would one day be able to bring herself to look at him again and his children would not turn away in horror from the monster that war had made of their daddy.

But this war had made far more monstrous creatures of the men who fought it, than any war before. Wright and Jones would know till their dying day, safely in their beds as it happens, that there could be no reconstructive surgery to heal and disguise the internal wounds inflicted on the soldiers. They would go on bleeding for the rest of their lives. They would see the atrocities that men were capable of inflicting on one another and on the innocent women and children, in their dreams. They would bear the guilt of their generation and be ashamed in front of their children and grandchildren. They would know that one day in the twenty-first century the world realized that there was no justification for seeing your fellow man as less than human, less than you are. Never again would soldiers follow orders to destroy and obliterate other races from the face of the earth. At least Wright and Jones would have been part of that realization and they would be there to tell the world what had made this war, at this time, on this God-forsaken battlefield the last to be waged on planet earth.

Agent (US)	a foreign national, who has been recruited by a staff case officer from an intelligence service to perform clandestine missions
AK-47	the 47 is only the first in a long line of weapons in the Kalashnikov family, designed in 1947. It was replaced by the AK-74 in 1974 in the Soviet army, but obviously, many survive.
Appendix the	the tower in Lubyanka that houses the KGB's most sensitive departments
Assault rifle	a weapon that fires both automatic and semi-automatic and uses medium-powered ammunition
Automatic	pull the trigger and hold it, and the bullets keep flying
Bang and burn	demolition and sabotage operations
Black operations	clandestine operations not traceable to the organization carrying them out
Bolt action	a bolt on top of the rifle replaces the slide of the pump action. WWII Mausers and Mauser carbines, British Enfields, French MAS rifles, Japanese Arisakas, Russian Moisin-Nagants and American Springfields have this action
Bona fides	an operative's true identity, affiliation, or intention

Cam-car	a vehicle equipped with a concealed camera
Camp the (also Camp Swampy)	a nickname for the CIA's secret domestic training base
Car chase	obligatory high speed chase
Casino	a useful location for the rich and powerful to meet and plot
Centre the	Russian intelligence headquarters in Moscow
Cheka	Russian secret police founded in 1917 to serve the Bolshevik Party; one of the many forerunners of the KGB
CIA	Central Intelligence Agency of the United States conducts foreign intelligence collection, covert action, and counterintelligence operations abroad and gives final intelligence to government
Clandestine operation	a secret intelligence operation
clip	a piece of metal which is pre-loaded with ammunition, then inserted into the weapon
Close protection officer	body guard
Code	a system used to disguise a message by use of a cipher, number, symbol etc
Compromised	when an operation or agent is uncovered
Dead letter drop	a secret location where materials can be left to be collected by another agent

Defector   a person with intelligence value who
                        volunteers to work for another
                        intelligence service

Drug barons   major villains, usually from Columbia or
                        Afghanistan, responsible for the world
                        wide distribution of hard drugs from their
                        source

Handguns   pistols and revolvers

Henchmen   most villains have at least one or two
                        trained thugs as protection, some have
                        private armies

KGB   intelligence and security service of the
                        U.S.S.R. during the Cold War, disbanded
                        in 1991

Legend (cover)   the complete cover story developed for
                        an operative

Lever action   some rifles have cocking handles
                        underneath the gun in the trigger area.
                        After the shot, the lever is pulled down
                        and forward, putting another bullet in the
                        chamber and cocking the weapon.

Lubyanka   the prison on Dzerzhinsky Square in
                        Moscow that is the traditional
                        headquarters of the Soviet intelligence
                        services. Now occupied by the FSB

Magazine	ammunition can be pre-loaded into a metal housing (magazine), then inserted into the weapon
MI5	British domestic and foreign counterintelligence service responsible for national internal security.
MI6	British foreign intelligence service.
Microdot	a photographic reduction of a secret message so small it can fit under a full stop
Mole	a human plant in an intelligence service
Operative	an intelligence officer or agent operating in the field
Profile	every known aspect of an operative's or a target's physical and psychological behaviour
Pump action	on shotguns and inexpensive single-shot rifles, a grip at the front of the gun, under the barrel, slides along a track. After firing, the shooter pulls the grip back toward him/herself, ejecting the shell, cocking the weapon and loading a round
Rabbit	the target in a surveillance operation

Revolver	revolvers have cylinders with six bullets
Round	the three pieces that go into a gun The shell, the propellant(gunpowder) and the bullet. The bullet goes toward the target. The shell is ejected
Safe house	a flat, hotel room, or other similar site considered safe for use by operatives
SB	Special Branch; usually the national internal security and domestic counterintelligence service
Secret writing	any technique employing invisible messages hidden in or on ordinary materials
Security service	a country's internal counterintelligence service
Semi-automatic	pull the trigger and the gun fires one bullet, then loads another bullet by itself and cocks the gun
Sensing device	a technical sensor designed to react to a concealed mark, chemical compound, or passive element
Single-shot	shoots one round at a time
Sinister	suspicious
Spoofing	deceiving the observer into believing that an operation has gone bad when, in fact, it has been put into another compartment
Spook	spy or agent
Stasi	East German State Security; including internal security, counterintelligence, and foreign intelligence collection

Sub machine guns   personal weapons that fire pistol ammunition automatically and are carried by one shooter. They have a short range, but fast delivery. The famous Tommy Gun was a submachine gun; so is the Russian PPSH-41, the original Uzi, the Sten and the Sterling

Ultimatum   a demand issued, which if not met will be followed by serious consequences

World Domination   the aim of many villains who have seemingly unlimited resources to achieve their ends

CHICK-LIT

It is extraordinary really, how many genres of contemporary fiction there are, and how many continue to emerge. Technically, chick-lit (chic-lit) is a sub-genre of romance, but when it emerged in the 1990s, it was such a breath of fresh air, and such a reflection of the changes in the attitudes of contemporary western society that it quickly merited shelf-space of its own. Young men were being served by the likes of authors Nick Hornby and Ben Elton and their works were already being described as 'lad-lit'.

Young women no longer found that traditional romantic fiction mirrored their experiences of love and life in the late twentieth century, especially if the life was that of twenty-something career girl, living in a major city (usually London or Manhattan). This readership was made up of the have-it-all girls who had been promised glamorous careers, handsome lovers, satisfying sex lives, and a happy ending. Then, at the right time, they would find true love, marry, have perfect babies, employ Mary Poppins and settle down with a house in the country and a flat in town. Of course, dream lives are notoriously difficult to pull off, and the successful authors of chick-lit tended to take an ironic tone when they described the hapless adventures of Izzy, and Imo, Caz and Maz and Mo, and their ilk, in pursuit of happiness.

Although chick-lit did not start out as formula fiction, the surprise arrival at the top of the best-sellers list of this vibrant new genre immediately spawned a hundred read-a-likes. The defining chick-lit title of the noughties is probably *Bridget Jones' Diary* by Helen Fielding. Perhaps one of the reasons that this genre took the bookstores by storm is the quality of the writing. Bridget Jones had started life as a regular satirical feature in a quality broadsheet newspaper, and readers followed Bridget's adventures in real time. Helen Fielding was already an accomplished writer and journalist with well-honed powers of observation and that was evident in the creation of the lovely Bridget. Other highly successful authors include Marian Keyes and Sophie Kinsella author of the Shopaholic series. Readers love to recognise themselves or their friends, or grown-up offspring in the characters and are able to laugh and cry with them.

As the twenty-somethings slide inexorably towards being thirty-somethings the genre has grown up with them, spawning 'mum-lit' for example, in which the hapless heroines become yummy-mummies and deal with the inevitable trials and disappointments of juggling young families and mislaid ambitions. Inevitably, what started as a popular publishing has become established in the intervening period and the book trade also talks of 'chiction', which includes more general female fiction and works of recognised literary merit like those of Jane Austen or the Brontes. Actually chick-lit is both a new genre and a new definition of an established one. It could be argued that *Cold Comfort Farm* was the chick-lit of its day, or the novels of Nancy Mitford of hers.

So what are the defining characteristics of chick-lit that distinguish it from general fiction and the romantic fiction of old. If you decide to write in this style, it is worth, as always, reading as many as possible of the titles that will undoubtedly be available in your local bookstore or public library, to get your eye in, as it were.

You will quickly realise that this style of writing can rapidly become passé, with its constant product placement and references to fashion labels and brand names. Think *Sex and the City*, which also began life as a newspaper column of course, and Carrie Bradshaw's obsession with Manolo Blahnik and Cosmopolitans.

It is worth scanning the glossy fashion magazines for popular names and trends and fashions in food and drink. The chick-lit of the 90s probably did more for the sales of Chardonnay than any other form of publicity. If you can afford it, and are young enough, nothing beats first hand research, and the listings magazines of major cities will tell you which restaurants, bars and entertainments are fashionable. Your text will be sprinkled judiciously with these references, as your heroines go out about their busy lives.

You will also need to have a good ear for contemporary vernacular, to write the convincing dialogue that is essential.

Heroines of chick-lit tend to have media-friendly jobs, like publishing, television, public relations or the music business and they will live in apartments, either alone or shared with a kindred spirit. If you are not familiar with the jargon and technical terminology of these businesses, it is worth asking a friendly company if you can shadow someone for a day, who has the real life position you have chosen for your heroine. (They can only say no!) The rules of dating, not to mention the disasters, feature heavily in this genre and they change all the time, so try to talk to singletons in the right age group, if you are not your own perfect role model. They are your potential readers and there is nothing more off-putting to them than a jarring word, or a piece of outdated slang. The nineties were the heyday of *Men are from Mars, Women are from Venus, The Rules* and such horrors as speed dating! Internet speed dating is still popular and might yield inspiration for a plot. And now to sex, which features both frequently and graphically in this genre. If you don't feel that you can write about it without embarrassment, this might not be the genre for you.

Don't be deceived into believing that because these novels are fairly light and superficial in tone, they are not carefully crafted. The same rules of careful characterisation and plotting apply here, and if the tone is to strike a chord with the readership you will need to pay close attention to keeping the style tight and witty. Puns, and clever titling are strong elements in successful chick-lit and this is nothing like as easy to achieve as one might imagine. Don't overdo the irony, you must be genuinely fond of your protagonists and the reader will be too. Use your character charts to create credible characters and keep them acting in character. A little serious pathos in your story will create contrast with the upbeat frothiness of the normal chick-lit style, and you need to have the courage of your confections to carry it off, but do allow your cast of characters to end their adventures happily, with no real harm done.

To summarize as Bridget might say herself; Characters: tengood, puns -12, v.bad; shags every ten pages – excellent!

Beginnings

1. Meg woke up with a start, as the alarm screamed in her left ear. Simultaneously, her mobile rang beside the bed and someone or something was pounding hard at the inside of her head. This wasn't as surprising as it might seem at first, when she remembered, the second jug of Sangria. Actually, she loathed Sangria, but it seemed that she had forgotten that,

caught as she had been like a rabbit in the headlamps of Ted's dark gaze. Thank God, she had managed to find her way home. Someone must have put her in a cab. The mobile had now given up, but was bleeping weakly and intermittently at her, and the alarm had upped its game to shrieking demandingly. As she switched them both off, and sank back into the blessed silence of her soft pillows, she heard the sound of water running somewhere, followed by the flush of the cistern.

That couldn't be right; she lived alone! Did burglars break into the homes of innocent people with terrible headaches, at crack of dawn to wash their hands? Meg crawled out of bed dragging the Egyptian cotton sheet with her and wrapping it around her naked (but even though she said so herself, buff body.) The room tilted unhelpfully as she tottered uncertainly towards the door. Meg picked up the baseball bat, in one hand and clutching the sheet around her, opened the bathroom door with a jerk. "Argh!" shrieked Meg, and the tall, dark, naked burglar cleaning his teeth at her basin, in unison. As Meg raised the baseball bat, Ted moved towards her and she lost her grip on the sheet. They stood together, nose to nose, naked and surprised.

Ted might well think that he had gone home with a bunny-boiler and that she now planned to brain him. But of the two, Meg was the more shocked, As the message that this was no ordinary burglar, that indeed this was Ted, the Ted, for whom she had poisoned her liver last night, and that he had evidently slept somewhere in the tiny flat, finally reached her pickled brain, she was somewhat concerned to think that it might have been in her bed. She was suddenly outraged to think that he had been so certain that he would go home with her that he happened to have his toothbrush with him. This bordered on the presumptuous. The fact that she and Sian had been planning 'the seduction of Ted' for months, was of no consequence, he hadn't known that.

"Put down that toothbrush," she said, in what she hoped was her best police procedural manner. "Not until you put down that bat," said Ted without missing a beat…

2. Kaz manoeuvred her way passed the teetering pile of washing up in the sink and turned on the tap. It really was time they had a bit of a cleaning fest, she thought, they had been reduced to drinking out of eggcups last night, and it was so difficult to keep track of the recommended number of units when one was not using standard measures. She filled the kettle and set it to boil. Spooning coffee into the cafetiere and searching fruitlessly for a mug, she settled upon a travel mug that had been in her Christmas stocking and waited patiently for the kettle to boil.

That of course was disastrous and she grew more and more impatient as the seconds ticked by. She tuned the radio to the morning news programme and pretended that she didn't care whether the kettle boiled or not. When this did not speed things up, she went back to the bedroom to find something to wear. Opening the wardrobe she was faced with a row of sad and empty hangers.

Somehow every stitch of clothing she possessed had hurled itself around the room to land in heaps on chairs and the floor. She rummaged about in the nearest pile and came up with a smart little Chanel skirt. Further investigations yielded a cream silk shirt and her favourite pair of Jimmy Choos. Examining her long legs in the mirror, she decided that a trip to the salon for a wax job should take priority in her busy day, but that her legs could take the skirt, without the fag of finding tights in the pile next to the laundry basket.

Her outfit selected, she returned to the kitchen and her coffee with a light heart. Somehow, she had managed to get up in time to shower, wash and straighten her blond bob and make-up her face, this morning, so she was ahead of the game. Her self-congratulatory mood took a bit of a dive as she picked up her mail from the hall and glanced at her credit card statement. But all in all it looked like being a butter-side up day. The message on her answer-phone was an unwelcome surprise therefore. She didn't recognise the voice but the message was clear, she was no longer employed at *Elan* magazine...

3. He couldn't get her out of his head, the girl with the brightest smile he had seen in a long while. Victoria Beckham had made it unfashionable to smile; pouting was the expression of choice for this year's crop of new hotties. Seb was perfectly aware that this description was un-pc and demeaned women and the men who described them in such terms. But since the thought police had not yet signed in for the morning shift, he felt that in the privacy of his own head he could think what he damn well liked. Anyway back to Charlie, she was just gorgeous. Sure, she had the latest clothes, and she filled them very nicely indeed, and he could tell that the hair and makeup were the work of Jai at GHD, none better, and not cheap. But there were dozens of girls in the club last night, with the same unofficial stylists and none of them had caught his eye the way that Charlie had.

Actually, he heard her before he saw her, that soft, deep

cultivated voice, talking discreetly into her mobile. She had shown the good manners to take the call away from the table where she had been joined a group of guys and girls, old friends by the look of things. He had asked the barman if she was a regular at the club, hoping for some inside gen, to put him at an advantage when he introduced himself. Girls who looked like her needed to be flattered by the idea that enquiries had been made. But Guy didn't know her so he had had to go in cold. He tried catching her eye but she seemed to be actually interested in what her friend was saying, and not looking around for a better prospect. It seemed that only the direct approach would do.

He bought a bottle of house red and holding the two glasses in his right hand, sauntered over to her table. She smiled when he tapped her on the shoulder, and invited him to join them, introducing herself and her friends without a second thought.

She laughed when he produced the wine. " You didn't need that," she said with a smile that reached her eyes, I was so hoping that you would come over and speak to me, otherwise I would have to have come to you...

4. Lucy gazed longingly at the dress in the window. It was one of those swanky couturiers where there was just one incredible model softly lit, calling to innocent passers-by like Lucy.

It was no good her gazing, her credit card was maxed out, and who was she kidding, size O was not a possibility for her as long as there was one Krispy Kreme doughnut left in the world.

Lucy had recently given up smoking, (good) and her

personal smoke free therapist had assured her that she would not gain any weight. This of course was true, as long as each unsmoked Marlboro Light was not replaced by an eaten Krispy Kreme. (bad)

Her lunch hour was nearly over anyway and she had an afternoon of leering from her disgusting boss to avoid. The way he leaned over her chair to look down her front whenever he passed her pod, made her flesh crawl. She had taken to staring resolutely at his crotch in the hope that he would feel as uncomfortable as she did when he leered. Jack said this would just encourage him and she should just give him a swift kick, but she had waited for years to get into the music business and she wasn't about to let this sleaze ball drive her out. She was fairly certain that kicking one's co-workers was a dismissible offence.

She was contemplating this gloomy prospect as she entered into the quadrant of the revolving door and made ready to push. Suddenly she was spinning round in the glass box and her scarf, was trapped, Isadora fashion, in the door. She banged helplessly like a black and white movie heroine on the partition, and he looked over his shoulder and stopped the door. To her chagrin, he was laughing. As she untangled her scarf she turned to him in outrage.

"How can you behave so irresponsibly in a revolving door?" she snapped, "I might have been strangled." He laughed again and she couldn't help admiring the way his eyes crinkled at the corners.

"You could have just taken it off," he suggested. "Insufficiently contrite and insufferably correct," she replied and stalked off towards the lift...

5. Mary and Sal had been friends since school and neither man nor money could make them cancel their weekly meeting, well not money anyway. The dissection of every aspect of their work and love lives was essential to the successful conduct of both. Neither could make a move without a full analysis of every event from every angle and their opinions were better informed by the several bottles of Chardonnay that must be consumed during the evening.

They were currently at a bottle and a half stage, and Mary had just ordered fat fries and mayonnaise to soak up the alcohol, as was there wont. Sal, had just described the daily exchange of lust-laden glances that she was enjoying with Jason from accounts.

Mary had advanced the opinion that they would almost certainly be engaged by the time of the office Christmas party. Mary had in turn just explained why she was still prepared to wait for Tim's call, although it was now six weeks since their 'night of passion'. Sal agreed completely, taking into account the fact that he may have lost her number, and that his jacket had probably been locked in the dry cleaner during the refurbishment of the shop after a small fire, and that by the time he had been able to collect it and discover the number in the top pocket he had been too embarrassed to call. Both girls were certain that Jason and Tim would get on like a house on fire, when they reached the couples having dinner together phase of their relationships.

It could be said to be a bit of a disappointment then, when as they stumbled towards the cab rank, clinging to one another for support, they encountered the lads themselves coming out of the club, hand in hand...

Endings

1. I'm a relationship girl. I glide seamlessly from one affiliation to the next, with the ease of a gazelle leaping over tree trunks and bushes. Unlike the gazelle however, I have on occasion been known to leave a few broken hearts in my wake. So when I woke up and found a text message, on my top of the range Blackberry, from my boyfriend of six months, excusing himself from our steady co-habitational dalliance it came as a bit of a shock.

"Hi Babe, thank you for arranging the meeting with Jan, went well. Have decided to take her up on the offer to head up Phoenix branch of KND, so will be leaving tomorrow morning (flying business class!) Please forward my mail to Jan's apartment in USA. You've been great and everything.

Thanks. P. xx"

It was not hard to visualize the scene; Jan Greentree had been a client of mine at the gallery. Your typical high flying, immaculately turned out, brimming with confidence American business woman. Not only did she have an eclectic taste in nude sculpture, but was cute and friendly and insisted that we went out for a cocktail to seal the sale. A number of cosmopolitans and a bottle of Pinot Grigio later, and I felt sufficiently relaxed and loose-tongued to tell her the story of Parker's and my relationship.

When we met, I was in a two-year relationship with Mike, a music producer. I had been totally swept up in Mike's glitzy world of lunchtime cruises down the Thames, drinks and free albums. Unfortunately for Mike, these important functions were also a hot bed for young schmoozers from every advertising company in London. Parker's dynamic personality just blew me away, unfortunately for Mike it also blew our relationship out of the water, as I slid from his arms on one side of the slowly chugging barge, to Parker's equally toned, but bronzed arms on the other.

We did not emerge from between the silk sheets of my four poster bed for the next three weeks. As I said before, I am a relationship girl, so once I had hooked my fish, I made sure that he was not going to flop his way off the deck and back into the sea. I was on the verge of telling Jan about how I had cunningly manoeuvred Parker and I into my dream flat in Notting Hill after only two months together, when I noticed her attention had wandered to the blonde 19 year-old executive hottie at the bar. Rather than berate her for not being gripped by my fascinating story of a 21st century romance, I gave her an understanding nod and drained my glass of wine, before leaving her to sidle up to him and lament how her companion had just been called away unexpectedly.

It turns out that Jan goes home alone less often than I do. Following our original cocktail night we became partners in crime on a weekly basis. Fun though it was to play wingman for Jan, a few months on, and I had tired of making swift exits halfway through conversations and told Jan that Parker was jealous of my evenings out and wanted me all to himself. She didn't take it very well and our friendship fizzled out as quickly as it had started.

When I sent my boyfriend into her clutches last night, I honestly believed that all had been forgiven. Parker did not receive the pay rise he had been aiming for at AD14, and the resultant sulk period went on for three weeks solidly. Not even my skimpiest outfits could lift his mood. I struck on the idea of calling Jan when we had not had sex for the sixth day in a row and I was terminally bored with TV reruns of Doctor Who. She had been sweet as sugar on the phone and seemed pleased to help out, "I can't wait meet him, will you be joining us?" My decision to let him go alone for professional reasons was probably a mistake!

2. Sophie's long locks looked becomingly dishevelled as she stepped out of the white Austin Tourer. Her pale, diaphanous, drop-waisted summer dress complemented her spotless elegant car. It was a mistake for Sophie to try to restore her golden strands to its chignon whilst in the middle of any other action, and in a characteristic move she misjudged the width of the running board and fell face down into a puddle. Mud and white chiffon never make good company. She looked more like the side wall of a tire than anything else. All that hard work and expense to create the right image for Lady Windermere, her future mother-in-law!

"Oh bother", muttered Sophie, dabbing hopelessly at the mud stains. "Peter my darling, what am I to do?" Peter had emerged from the house just in time to see the event. He looked at her - his handsome face expressed utter contempt in all its aquiline length. His heavily hooded eyes looked down his slightly hooked nose and his full lips curled. "Not a thing darling", he said sardonically, "it is just as well if Mother sees you for what you are – a bit of a clumsy muddle. No doubt she will learn to love you as I do." "How can you love me Peter, when I am so very useless?" said Sophie, her voice going flat and her eyes losing their sparkle. "It is for the wonderful possibilities my darling, underneath all that clobber - you are a fabulous IT girl", he said, his voice oozing charm and warmth. "This time next year you will be a very different – a lady in fact."

His answer was her epiphany. It was suddenly clear how Peter, the handsome and elegant aristocrat could love her, imperfections and all. To him it was the excitement of taming her wild rebellious spirit, transforming her into a fashion drone. He knew how very much she loved him and how much she wanted to make this brilliant match work. This time next year she would be thinner and more beautiful; disciplined in what she said and ate, able to mix with the right set. There would be no more picnics on the beach in the summer rain, no more chocolate feasts with the gang and Raggedy Anne would be re-homed. No more Sophie.

Suddenly she ran up to Peter and gave him a long, lingering, muddy kiss. Then pressed the car keys into his hand, turned and jumped onto Freddie's bike, calling over her shoulder, "Tell Freddie I will return it tomorrow." "Where are you going Sophie, and what do I tell Mother?" Peter roared after her. Sophie paused for a moment, putting one foot on the ground and leaving the other on the pedal. Not even turning around she replied quietly, "Tell her you discovered that Sophie is 'all that clobber' and that you are well out of it." The last time he saw Sophie, she was obscured by a cloud of dust and her hair was flying behind her.

3. Annette paused in emptying the washing machine and thought, I do not care what the ads say, coloured clothes do not get clean at 30 degrees. It's all very well to want to minimize our carbon footprints, but I cannot send Sam to school with spots on his sweater. I will just have to make up for it by not heating the utility room anymore.

The church bells rang in the valley, reminding Annette that

the Miller wedding had started. She visualised the bride floating down the aisle, stopping just in front of her flower arrangement. The cream roses, chrysanthemums and lilies set against the variegated foliage smelt heavenly and looked divine. The bowers of elderflower and crab apple blossoms added a touch of country to the otherwise suburban church setting.

I am actually doing weddings for the likes of the Millers – I have arrived, thought Annette. It could not be denied, providing arrangements of locally grown cottage blooms for family celebrations and bereavements was finally catching on. I may not put Amsterdam out of business but 'Daisy Chain' is a force to be reckoned with and will pay me enough to live on. Annette thought of her despair and loneliness only six months before. Frank had run off with that evil twenty-four-year old, Tracey. How tedious it was to have to be brave and cheerful to friends, neighbours and children. Why don't my eyes look alluringly vulnerable when I cry?

Thinking back, the first step in the right direction had been the decision to sell Paddocks and buy outright the little two-bedroom semi in the middle of town. The traffic could be noisy, but it was also company, even if only vicariously. The tiny south facing walled garden was an enormous compensation for loss of space and a respectable postcode. To think she had once lived in W11, even if she had shared with four other girls. She wondered now why she had been so keen to give up her independence to settle down with Frank. What happened to the carefree Chardonnay quaffing girl of only a few short years ago?

Annette hummed quietly as she stuffed the clothes into the drier and poured herself a large glass of white wine, promising herself that from tomorrow she would always hang the clothes out of doors.

4. "The weather will continue to be cool and dry, with anti-cyclonic highs for most of the coming week" reported the attractive meteorologist, on a well-known Sky TV channel.

"So what has happened to global warming, floods and rains?" muttered Simon to himself, squirming on the sofa and disturbing the head that was resting so comfortably on his shoulder.

Lifting her head slightly, Charity laughed, "I am sure they will discover this is just another manifestation of it. One season deluges, the next drought, it is all about extremes."

"Well, I am not sure that the weather is all that different from the way it used to be. I can remember my father being worried about having enough rain for the wheat crop or enough sun to cut the hay. People always idealise the past."

Charity nodded, "Well that is for the best, happy memories are sustaining during tough times. They remind us that things can get better. Bad memories only make one bitter and negative." And to herself, Charity thought, Simon and I must only remember the good times and let the bad times go.

The scene was one of ordinary domestic contentment, the two curled up on a worn, rather crumpled sofa. There were half empty wine glasses on the floor and the lingering smells of roast chicken pervaded the house. Jet lay on the mat in front of the fireplace, occasionally rolling over with a snuffle and a sigh.

Simon looked relaxed for the first time in weeks. It was finally over. Simon leaned forward and kissed the top of Charity's head and said, "I hope that Tim is resting in peace. I wish that he could know how much we loved him and will always think of him."

Suddenly the heavens opened and hail stones the size of peas came pouring down.

5. The wedding was gorgeous, we all agreed, and Jaz looked absolutely fabulous and so happy! I hadn't realised how thin she had got to fit into that dress until I saw her coming up the aisle. She looked positively Lindsay Lohan, but hopefully properly underpinned.

I wore my favourite Baski gown and heels so high I was almost on a level with the pulpit. There must have been fifty-thousand dollars worth of designer outfits on the bride's side alone and the men didn't look too shabby either. Jaz's mum cried, but that was to be expected and her baby brother looked so cute dressed as Frodo the ring-bearer. There was a nasty moment when he went head over heels as he stood on his own furry feet, but fortunately Cally took the catch when the ring sailed towards the font, like the one ring to rule them, heading for the crack of doom. Talking about doom, the groom's mum didn't look too happy to see her boy fall into the clutches of a scheming minx, who was obviously no better than she should be.

She had confided to me over a fifth dry sherry that she had never liked Jaz, and couldn't understand why I had let her steal Sol away from me. She thought I was being very brave and noble, and I would always be welcome in her home, since I was more like a daughter to her than that woman would ever be.

I don't know how much she took in, but I tried to explain that it was I who had introduced the happy couple, and that whilst I thought that they were perfect for one another and loved both dearly, I would rather have my gel sculpted nails ripped from my pianist's fingers and walk in a hand knitted cardigan through the hallowed portals of Harvey Niks than be married to Sol. We just wouldn't have done well together and besides it was much better all round that the baby's parents be married to one another.

Advertising
Alarm clock
Alcohol
Answer Phone
Apartment
Apartment
 (1 bedroom
 1 bathroom,
 living room
 and kitchenette)
Aristocrats

Bar
Best Friend
Best gay friend
Best Mate

Career
Cars
Celeb
Cellphone/mobile
Cigarettes – Marlboro Lights
Club
Coffee/Coffee Shop
Confidence
Country weekends

Date
Diet
Diet Coke

Emotional archaeology
Emotional post mortem
Engaged

Fake Tan
Fashion
Flirting
Flowers

Girlfriend/Boyfriend

Hangover
Harvey Nichols
Hottie

It girl

Landline

Magazines
Married
Mates
Mothers
Music Business

Naked

Party
Phone Numbers
Pinot Grigio
Pizza
Plus one
Polo
Pub
Public relations
Publishing

Relationship

Saks Fifth Avenue
Self help
Sex
Shag
Shoes
Singelton
Single
Skiing
Small Children
Sober
Sofa
Sushi

Uberbabe
Urban

Wonderbra
Yummy Mummy

MEMOIR

If chick-lit was the new genre of the nineties and the eco-thriller looks set to make its mark in the future, the genre which has captured the popular imagination of the reading public and made the book store tills go 'kerching' in the first decade of the noughties, is personal memoir. There are no sample stories to inspire you here and no buzzwords, as both belong with fiction and this genre is very much non-fiction; or it should be.

Personal memoir is much less daunting to write than autobiography, as it can be very much shorter and can deal with any aspect of, or period in, or life-changing event in a person's life. In previous generations, only the famous and celebrated have been considered to have led exciting or important enough lives to merit publication. Even in our own time, celebrities of any calibre seem to publish the story of their lives, even if they are only twenty-five years old. However, many so-called ordinary people have fascinating or shocking periods in their lives, triumphing over adversity and surviving the most damaging of childhoods and adolescences. Readers are moved and inspired by accounts of abused children who have been diminished almost to the point of disappearance and rebuilt their adult lives with outstanding courage and determination. This branch of memoir is known as Misery Memoir in the trade, or as some wag has dubbed it 'Cryography'.

However you don't have to have suffered to have a tale to tell. In the past, travel memoirs were exceptionally popular and in a world where there are few places to which we cannot travel, many people have extraordinary adventures to share. Perhaps you have devoted a part of your life to a particular cause or charity, or have been in public service, or had a special interest in the arts or science. Your memories of those events can be of interest and inspiration to other people. But in any event, our watchwords are 'just write', and this applies just as much to personal reminiscence as to fiction. A record of this kind can be therapeutic to write if only for yourself, but it can also be immensely valuable and illuminating for your family and for future generations. The war time experiences of ordinary men and women have led historians to a much greater understanding of real events during the two world wars. The diaries or memoirs of ordinary soldiers too, teach us something about ourselves as a society. Diaries discovered in attics have always fascinated readers, even when they describe the humdrum events of daily life.

If you think that you have a story to tell, it is a good idea to write a brief overall outline for yourself. You can use the character chart we use when inventing fictional characters to examine your own traits and foibles and those of others in your story. Use the plotline to record times and dates as accurately as you can, it is helpful to put your memories in order. Try to keep it simple, without embellishment, and try too to avoid the distortions that happen to all of us when we tell and retell real-life events.

If others are involved in your memoir and you have uncomfortable things to say about them, consider changing their names and physical descriptions in print. You do not want to end up in a libel court because in the event, you and another have different memories of the same story and neither can prove the veracity of their version. You can also publish under a pseudonym, if you do not want very private matters to generate unwelcome press attention.

Children's Books

We would all like to be JK Rowling who has enjoyed such outstanding success with the Harry Potter books. She has contributed immeasurably to the enjoyment of a generation of readers, young and old alike, and she has introduced many young people to the matchless pleasure of reading. Her own story is the stuff of legend; the single mother writing in coffee shops with her baby in the buggy beside her; the rejection letters and the final acceptance and publication of the first book, and the rest as they say is history. It must be said that her early experience is not unusual, but the unprecedented worldwide success of her books is almost unique.

She is immensely talented and original as an author, but so are many others, so it is advisable not to expect too much if children's fiction is your chosen genre. There are literally thousands of new children's books published every year, for every age group, illustrated and narrative, paperback and hardback. It would not be possible here to sample every kind fairly so this part is limited to some general advice to would-be authors.

Many of us tell stories to our children and grandchildren that are much loved and become part of the oral history of our families. Write them down, and perhaps invite family members to add to them or to provide illustration. They can become treasured family documents.

If you are intent on general publication, do some research into the appropriate levels of understanding of words and concepts for your chosen age group. Your local children's librarian will be able to help you. The information you glean will be priceless if it helps you write in a style and with a vocabulary that resonates with your young readers. Don't be discouraged if you are at first rejected. The sheer number of titles offered to publishers each week makes selection very difficult and they may be looking for a particular genre to suit a gap in their lists. Visit the websites of publishers you would like to approach, or write and ask for a catalogue of their books. Make sure that your work fits well with the kind of book that they publish before submitting your manuscript. At the time of writing, publishers admit to looking for good quality adventure stories for young adult males and really contemporary fiction that reflects the experiences of boys and girls growing up in our multicultural society.

Getting it out there

Publishing can seem a mysterious and daunting world to the first time author, so the following brief advice is aimed at introducing the virgin author to the arcane secrets of this dark art.

Publishers are the specialist intermediaries between the writer and the book trade and, most importantly, the reader. It is their job to choose or commission titles that will add to the literature available to the reader to entertain, educate or inform and to make a profit. There are many different specialist houses that will publish academic work or poetry, fiction or cookery, art or literary fiction, general non-fiction or travel and so on. The most comprehensive listing of publishers and their specialities is to be found in the *Writers and Artists Yearbook* in the UK, which is updated annually. Similar indispensable volumes exist in most countries. Do take note of publisher's instructions, with regard to submissions. If they say that they don't consider unsolicited manuscripts, don't send them yours in a large brown parcel. Instead send a brief outline of your book with perhaps a sample chapter if they ask for one. Be careful to research the right kind of publisher for your book and you will save yourself a lot of heartache and rejection.

The publisher takes the financial risk in publishing a title, including the cost of paper and print, marketing, sales, publicity and distribution. This is a considerable financial investment in each individual title. They will also take responsibility for preparing your text for print. That includes copy editing, checking the content, and correcting errors of fact, grammar, punctuation etc, and design of the book and the jacket. They employ specialist staff in all these areas to work on the books.

A commissioning editor, the person to whom you will send your submission, is responsible for selecting the books in the first instance and championing the book 'in-house'. He or she will prepare a synopsis and sales outline and 'sell' the book to the marketing and sales department who will estimate the number of copies they think the book will sell, if published. He or she will then work with the production and other departments to cost the book and set a reasonable retail price. This will include the cost of every aspect of the book's production and marketing against projected sales.

The commissioning editor will then be able to make you an offer of an advance against the sales of your book. This is yours regardless of whether the book sells all the copies printed or not. The experience and arithmetic of the publisher is paramount here. The aim is that all the copies printed will be sold and thereafter the author will get an agreed percentage of the cover price on every copy sold (a royalty), in every market, for as long as the book is in print.

Sometimes, publishers offer authors a flat fee, with no royalties. This will tend to be higher than an advance, but no further payments will be made regardless of the success or failure of the title. In either event if your book is chosen, the publisher will issue a contract, binding you and the house to certain things. You will be asked to guarantee that your work is original and non-libellous for example, and delivery dates and specifications are included, as well as royalty rates and mutual safeguards. Ask the publisher to go through it with you, and your own solicitor to look over it before you sign. The Society of Authors is immensely helpful to its authors in contractual matters and is inexpensive and easy to join.

The time that a book takes to produce from commissioning to publication varies from book to book, but the process is not a short one. During editing and design the team will be in constant touch with you and are there to help. Once the book goes to the printer, you will be contacted by publicity who may ask you to be involved in book tours and signings and interviews with the press. Your first task is to address your submission to the commissioning editor and be patient. You should receive an acknowledgment that they have received it fairly quickly, but it may take some time before you are accepted or rejected.

Many authors prefer to save the anguish of corresponding with publishers by employing an agent. Agents represent you with publishers and negotiate on your behalf for a percentage of your income from the book. They are specialists and know who to approach and how to present your book to the best advantage. The only drawback is finding an agent who is prepared to take you onto their books. There is a full list of literary agents on the Internet.

Some authors are taking advantage of the opportunities that the Internet offers to self-publish and this is worth considering if you are not wedded to the printed word in book form. Blogs and other writing forums also offer potential for new writers to reach an audience. You may have heard of e-books, which download to specialist readers, like mp3 players, but with a page turning facility that simulates the 'book' experience. Publishers will include ebook rights in their contracts.

A final word. Unless you wish to publish a limited edition for a small, exclusive market, perhaps a family history for example for family and friends, you don't need to pay someone to publish your book (known as vanity publishing). Resist advertisements that ask you to submit your work and then ask you to pay them. If your work is considered good enough to publish, then they should be paying you.